Farr Cottage

Back from America. The Farr Family Saga

Anita D. Boseman

Published in the United States of America

Brilliant Books Literary
137 Forest Park Lane Thomasville
North Carolina 27360 USA

ISBN:
Paperback: 979-8-88945-137-2
E-book: 979-8-88945-138-9

There are two people who deserve my deepest thanks: my dear, departed husband, Vann, for putting up with me while I wrote this book and the ones coming after it; and my sister, Carolyn, who is my biggest fan and preliminary editor. Funny, but for a writer I don't have the words to tell you how much you both mean to me!

I also want to stress that this book is a work of fiction, the people, places, and titles are all a product of my imagination. The history of Houston has been "adjusted" to fit the storyline, but to my beloved city and the state of Texas, my heart forever belongs to you.

Contents

The Inheritance

Melody Fitzhugh Farr – daughter of the late Charles Andrew Farr
and Evangeline Louis Fitzhugh

Lord Arthur Roland Farr – Viscount of Gibbons, cousin and guardian of Melody Fitzhugh Farr, lives in Farr Cottage, the family's ancestral home in Kent

Lord Alfred Oswin – lives at Aldwin House near Farr Cottage, son of Sir Alden Alfred Oswin and Lady Mayda Elizabeth Fritzwilliam

Nedda – housekeeper to Lord Arthur Farr in Farr Cottage

John – husband of Nedda and serves as driver, butler, gardener

Lily – day help at Farr Cottage, lives in the village

The Reverend Charles Paxton – Vicar of the local church Livia Paxton – wife of the vicar

Peter Jessup – Grandson of the vicar and owner of a computer services shop

The New World of Farr Cottage

Richard Arthur Farr – Fourth son of Arthur, fifteenth viscount of Gibbons; Melody's great-great grandfather

Lord Arthur Charles Farr – Fifteenth Viscount of Gibbons; Richard Farr's Father

Lady Annis Louis Farr – mother of Richard

Lord Harold Charles Farr – Sixteenth Viscount of Gibbons; oldest brother of Richard and inheritor of the estate and titles of the family upon the death of his father

Captain Roland Arthur Farr – Second brother of Richard Farr; regiment bound for India

The Reverend Edgar Charles Farr – Richard's third brother and the newly appointed vicar of the local church, a post a Farr has usually held

Lucinda Louise Langley (Lucy) – Wife of Richard Arthur Farr, and niece of Jeremy and Abbey Higgins; Melody's great-great grandmother

Abigail Johnson – Boarding house owner where Richard Farr lives when he first arrives in Houston, Texas

John "Big Red" Chadwick – cattleman and co-owner of Chadwick Ranch with his sister

Elbeth Chadwick – sister of John and wife of Doc Harris Doctor John Harris – husband to Elbeth Chadwick and

future founder of St. Luke's Anglican Hospital in Houston

Jeremy Higgins – Cattleman, friend, and mentor of Richard Farr

Abigail Montgomery Higgins – wife of Jeremy Higgins and aunt of Lucy Langley Farr

Annis Louise Farr – daughter of Richard Arthur Farr and Lucinda Louis Langley Farr; older sister of Melody's great grandfather

Avery Richard Farr – Son of Richard Arthur Farr and Lucinda Louis Langley Farr; Melody's great grandfather, younger brother to Annis Louise Farr

Interlude in London

Mrs. Jones – London house cook

Angie – Niece of Mrs. Jones who is often hired for day help when the London house is being used

The Inheritance

T he last train pulled into the station after dark. It was well past ten in the evening, and the only lights beyond the station were coming from the pub just down the street. There was no taxi, no one to meet the passengers or to porter the luggage. Melody Fitzhugh Farr stood alone with her suitcase.

Melody had been traveling for several days, or at least this was how it felt. She was originally from Houston, Texas, and the little train station in the one-lane village was a decided shrinking of her world. In addition, she had no idea where her cousin Arthur was, though she'd been told he would meet her.

A low rumble was heard in the distance and slowly gained in irritation as an aged car came to a halt at the foot of the station steps. A tall man emerged, and without a word to Melody, took her suitcase in hand. He opened the door on the wrong side and motioned for her to get in. She realized it was the passenger door when she remembered they drove on the wrong side in Britain.

Her case went into the trunk and the driver got back into the car. Past the pub and into the darkness, the man drove on without speaking. It was impossible to see anything but the road ahead, and it wasn't until the driver turned into a stone gate Melody realized they had been on a two-lane road. It had been so narrow, but the drive they turned onto was no wider than the car.

Suddenly, in the car's headlights, a dark stone edifice began to loom ahead. For the first time, the driver spoke. "Farr Cottage," was all he said. Melody had heard about Farr Cottage from the time she was a child. Her father's family had been British. A long time ago and once, when her grandfather had been in the army, her grandfather had passed through England on his way to the war in Europe.

He had gotten permission to travel, by train, to this area of England and the place where his ancestors had called home. He was the last and the first in several generations of American Farr's to see the Cottage. The only thing he said about it was in a letter mailed just a few days before he was killed, two days after the Normandy invasion.

It didn't look so small in the dark, but she didn't have much time to look at the outside. Before the car came to a stop, the front door opened and a plump lady in black stood in a pool of light. The driver opened her door and took her suitcase from the back.

"Come in, come in, it's too late to be outside. My name is Nedda and I am the housekeeper of Farr Cottage. My husband, John, will put your case in your room, but I am to take you into the kitchen and get you something to eat before you go up. This way please."

Nedda turned and Melody followed. The only light was in the entry and the rest of the room was in darkness. The gloom didn't extend to walls, but to a fuzzy emptiness which promised a larger room than what she had expected. Nedda opened a door, which again allowed light to spill forth and the whitewashed walls made the space much more cheerful than the main room. They went down a short hall, and the table of an eat-in kitchen came into view.

It was an old kitchen, but the appliances looked fairly new and it was incredibly clean. On the wood table, a plate sat with a napkin covering its contents. Nedda motioned for Melody to sit as she removed the napkin. A large metal tumbler was put in front of her and a pitcher of juice was brought from the refrigerator.

The plate had a generous slice of bread, some cheese, a slab of cold ham, and the juice was lemon squash. Nedda also supplied a plate of butter and some jam from the pantry which was at the end of the room. "Now, you eat and I will see about your bag. Wait here until I come back for you."

Before Melody could ask any questions, she was alone. What she really wanted was a bathroom, but since it hadn't been offered, she would have to wait. The bread was very tasty and the rest of the food was washed down with the lemon drink. She hadn't realized she was so hungry, but before long, it was finished. The bread must have been homemade and the jam was one she didn't recognize, but it was tart, and it offset the lovely yellow butter that went with it.

Nedda returned just as Melody was putting her plate and utensils in the sink. "Don't wash those, it's my job! Right now you need to come with me, this way."

Nedda opened a small door near the pantry and a narrow staircase could be seen in the glow of an overhead light. Melody followed the housekeeper up the stairs until they reached the next floor. It opened into a broad corridor, but then Nedda opened another door to an equally narrow set of stairs similar to the ones they had just climbed. These stairs led to a short corridor, which had several doors. One was open and Nedda pointed to it. "This is the bathroom and across from it is the toilet. If you need to use either, please do so now before I take you to your room."

Melody ducked into the toilet and, once inside, wondered about the aged facilities. Within minutes, she had finished and returned to the hall. Nedda was waiting for her and frowned. "I suppose you will want to bathe in the morning too. All right, the water will be hot enough by the time you wake up. Here is your room. There is a pitcher of water on the table and an extra blanket for your bed. I will close the door and recommend you don't leave your room until I come for you in the morning. Good night."

Before Melody had a chance to answer, the door closed, and the only sound was Nedda's shoes retreating down the corridor.

The room was small with a plank wood floor, single metal-frame bed, night table, and two-drawer dresser. A plain wooden chair sat under the single, high window in the room. There was a tiny mirror above the dresser and on it sat an old-fashioned pitcher and bowl. Melody saw her suitcase on the floor next to the bed.

She took her toiletry bag from the case and put it next to the pitcher. The water in it was as cold as the room, but filled almost to the top. The bedside table also sported an old wind-up alarm clock that ticked loudly. Melody looked around but did not see any place to hang her clothes. On the back of the door was a single hook which would have to do for now, but she had to remember to ask Nedda about it in the morning.

As tired as she was, she did not forget to say her nightly prayers. Melody took her prayer book from her purse, knelt on the wooden floor, and bowed her head. At the end of her prayers, she added the names of her cousin, Arthur Farr, Nedda, and Nedda's husband, John, to the list of those for whom she prayed. This was her way, praying for anyone and everyone who was a part of her daily life.

Teeth brushed, prayers said, a warm flannel nightgown on against the chill, and she was ready for bed. The sheets were cotton and very rough, the blanket was a little thin, but Melody was tired enough she was sure it wouldn't matter. The first time she got on the bed, the squeal of the springs made her think otherwise.

Melody turned to look out the small window while the springs on the bed screamed under her slight weight, and once in a relatively comfortable position, she lay as still as possible to keep the bed from objecting to her presence. She tried to quiet her mind in order for sleep to come, but it was beginning to prove difficult. In an effort to sleep, her mind plowed through the most recent past.

Her life had been very comfortable as she was growing up. Her grandfather, the one who had visited Farr Cottage during the war, had not made it back home. Little more than a month after the visit, he had been killed in France and the only mention of his visit was in a letter he had sent his young wife, Melody's grandmother. Her father had never known his father. He was a baby when the war started and the only picture he had of him was one taken when grandfather had been home on leave before being sent to England prior to the invasion. His mother had taken it with an old Brownie box camera and except for a couple of pictures his mother had, it was the extent of his knowledge of what his father looked like.

Her great-grandparents had moved her grandmother into the family home where they could help her raise their only grandchild.

Her parents were unable to help her and what she had expected would only be a few months turned into years. As her parents-in-law aged, she stayed on to help care for them. Her son, Melody's father, left for university from his mother's home and when he finished his studies, he returned to the same house.

He married Melody's mother, a Fitzhugh, and brought her to live in the family home. Melody was born there. Her grandmother died in the home, followed shortly by her father. Her mother had just passed in the last month.

Melody had gone to university and studied history, but once graduated, she was expected to return after receiving her Master's degree. By this time, her mother was sick and needed her care. It wasn't until her mother passed away she learned the contents of her father's will.

As the only child of an only child, she had thought the property would pass to her, but her father had used the old family lawyer to draw up his will and in the process, accepted the mind-set of yesteryear. Melody did inherit, but not until she was thirty. At twenty-eight, she had two years yet to wait. In the meantime, a search was conducted to find any living male relatives on the Farr side of her family, but the only one was a very distant cousin in England.

Mr. Lynch, the grandson of the lawyer who had drawn up her father's will, sat in the study, and explained the document and it's special provisions to her. "You are the sole inheritor, but because of the age clause, your money and property will be managed by the trustees at the bank. Each month you will receive a stipend and the expenses of running this house will be paid by the trust. If you were to marry before the age of thirty, permission from the trustees would need to be obtained or the trust resets to age thirty-five. I don't see any problem with getting their approval. They will, of course, do a thorough background check including a financial investigation on any prospective suitor to determine whether he is more interested in your inheritance or in you."

"If you decide you want to travel or anything of this nature, you will need to inform the trustees beforehand. Now, I have with me a letter sent by your guardian in England. I do not know the contents, but you are to read it in my presence. The reason for this will become apparent once it has been read."

He took a large envelope from his briefcase and handed it to Melody. She opened it and began to read:

Dear Miss Melody Fitzhugh Farr:

I have been informed your last parent has passed on and I am the only living male relative on the Farr side of the family who is over the age of majority. You have my deepest sympathy for your loss.

According to your father's wishes, it is my understanding the provisions of your father's will make it clear you are to have the guardianship of a male Farr as your manager until the appropriate age is reached. I therefore extend an invitation to you to come to my home where I may undertake the duties of your guardian.

It is also my understanding you have an advanced degree in History, although the particulars are unknown, which might be of use to me. The Farr family history is a lengthy one and it is my wish for it to be documented. If you will be under my roof as my ward, it would be convenient for you to undertake this work. If this is agreeable to you, please inform the attorney, and the arrangements for your travel will be made.

Regards,

Sir Arthur Roland Farr

Melody took the letter, put it back in the envelope, and drew out a picture. The man in the photo looked to be in his forties, had brown hair mixed with grey, and tended toward lean. He was well-dressed, was photographed before a grouping of what must have been old family portraits, and seemed to be near six feet tall. He was not smiling, but neither was he overly stern-looking. He was neither handsome nor distasteful, but really rather ordinary.

She replaced the photo with the letter and began to hand the package back to the lawyer. He put his hand up to stop her. "No, you keep it, but I do need an answer from you."

Melody thought about the letter. She had never traveled far, just to university and once to the state fair in Dallas. Texas was enough for her. Everything she could ever want or need was there. Even her university was close enough she could have driven back and forth each day, but her mother had wanted her to have the experience of college, so she had spent her undergraduate years in campus housing. Well, at least she would get to see her family's ancestral home.

She examined the outside of the plain envelope she held in her hands. "Please inform my cousin I will accept," she replied quietly.

Before she could change her mind, the attorney gave her another envelope. "You will find all of the things you will need for your trip inside. The application for a passport is in there and it needs to have a rush put on it. Your ticket, instructions, and a list of things to take with you are all there. I would judge the items will not take more than one suitcase and other things would probably be unnecessary, so go with what has been listed. If you have any questions, there is a number in the envelope where you can get some help and guidance."

She took the envelope, put it with the other, and looked to the attorney. "What about my house?"

Young Mr. Lynch put up a hand to stop her. "The trustees will continue to pay the upkeep of this property from the estate. The house will be closed while you are gone and it will be here when you return. Each month you will receive a stipend, allowance if you will, from the estate. The first such check is in this envelope." He reached into his suit jacket and removed it from his inner pocket.

Melody added it to the two she already held. "Does my guardian get paid for looking after me?"

The attorney nodded. "Yes, but the trustees are the ones who deal with this question and I don't know how much it will be. You can ask them. There number and contact information is in with your

15

first check. Now, this concludes our business. If you have no further questions, then good day."

She saw the man to the door. The next few days were very busy with passport applications, a visit to the trustee bank, and preparing the house to be closed. It was the visit with the bank that was the most interesting for Melody.

Texas had previously had a ban on branch banking. Until sometime in the 1980s, before she had been born, this had changed, and when it did, the bank her family had owned for almost one hundred years was bought by a larger bank. Her father had been on the board of the purchasing bank until he passed away, but a goodly portion of the family money had been made in banking and this was where it remained.

She knew where the trustee bank was, but had never needed to be in the main office since all of her contact had been through the local branch near the family home. The chrome and glass edifice in downtown was one of the many which graced the Houston skyline, but the marble lobby of the bank sounded hollow under her heels. The gentleman she had to meet was on one of the upper floors, and a secretary escorted her there.

Mr. Baldwin was a tall slender man of indeterminate years. He came out from behind his desk, shook her offered hand, and dismissed the secretary. The door to his room, however, remained open.

He sat down and opened a large file laid in front of him. "Now, I first wish to offer my condolences, on behalf of the bank, for your loss. There has been a long history between our banking family and yours, so it will be felt. The next thing we need to do is have you sign some paperwork having to do with the trust, which will manage your affairs until your thirtieth birthday. If you want a lawyer to look over these, please feel free to do so."

He took the sheaf of papers, bound with a legal looking blue back page, from the file and passed it to her. It was fairly easy to read. Since the shock of the will reading, she had done some research into the kinds of trusts that were written along the same lines as her father's, so she knew much of the verbiage and the meanings of various phrases used. After reading the document, the man told her where to sign.

While she was signing and initialing each page, the trustee explained the payments to her and her guardian. "You will receive, each month, a stipend. If you find it difficult to manage on what has been set aside, please let me know. I would rather you asked for an increase than to go into debt or, worse still, default on checks or a loan. As for your guardian, he has been offered a payment each month, but has declined. However, the payments he would have received will be put aside in case he changes his mind. Any questions?"

Melody thought about what he had said while she closed her pen and put it back in her purse. "I don't think so. You have covered everything very well. There is one other thing. I need a safety deposit box to put some things in before I go. I will not be taking most of the jewelry that passed to me from the women in my family, and there are some papers which need securing. Can you please show me were to get one here at the bank?"

Mr. Baldwin pressed a button on the communications console on his desk. Almost before he released it, his secretary was standing in the open door. "Please take Miss Farr to the basement so she can get a safety deposit box, and then wait for her there so you can see her out." He turned to Melody, and while he shook her hand, wished her a pleasant day and safe trip. "Please feel free to keep in contact will me at any time."

━━━◄◉►━━━

Sleep finally won over the tension and the objecting springs. Before long, however, a persistent knocking on her door woke her in the predawn hours.

It was Nedda, with a tenacious strong knock. "Get up, get up. Didn't you set your alarm? What did you suppose the clock was put there for, it's not for show. This house rises early so get up now. You have a half-hour to bathe and dress before you need to be in the kitchen for breakfast."

Melody took her bathrobe from the foot of the bed and put it over her flannel nightdress. She remembered the location of the toilet room and she took her things for a bath. The bathroom had an ancient claw-foot tub with dual taps. There was no shower, so her idea of washing her hair was not going to happen—at least, not until she had a way of mixing the hot and cold water with a hose of some sort. It took forever to fill the tub, and the hot water was not very hot nor was there much of it. She did get her bath though and it helped to ease some of the tension she felt.

Back in her room, she put the prescribed outfit on as per the instructions she had gotten in the packet of travel papers. The lawyer had told her there was a list of items she should pack and once she read it, it seemed she was to be dressed in nothing more colorful than black and white. It didn't bother her since she was still in mourning for her late mother, and the idea of color was not an issue.

On the list were three black skirts, mid-length, four white shirt-waist blouses with long sleeves, a black cardigan, black jacket, black coat, and two pair of "sensible shoes." The shoes were the most questionable. Since her sixteenth birthday, her mother and grandmother had insisted she be used to wearing heels. She had oxfords she had worn with her school uniform, but in the house, at church, or any event she would attend with her family, she was to wear stockings and heels.

When Melody went away to college, she learned the value of the lessons her mother and grandmother had taught her. While the rest of the girls were complaining about having to stand for long periods of time, she was quite comfortable in her heels. The other girls ran around the dorm in flip-flops or barefoot, but she was in heels or mules and never had problems with her feet. When they would all dress up for a party, she was the only girl who did not kick off her shoes at the first opportunity. Her family wanted her to be raised to be a lady, and this is what they got.

Dressed in the black skirt, white blouse, and wearing the cardigan against the chill, she found her way to the kitchen on the main floor. Walking on the carpeted part of the hall on the second floor, her heels made no sound, but once on either of the two stairways or the hall to the kitchen, her shoes could be heard on the stone or wood floors.

Nedda heard her coming and met her at the kitchen door. Behind her, sitting at the table, were Nedda's husband and another, younger woman. "What is the racket? Weren't you told to bring sensible shoes? Why would you ever think those could be called sensible?"

Melody looked down at her shoes, but Nedda wasn't finished. "You will need to get other shoes, but not today. John, my husband, has other work today and he can't take you to the village. But, tomorrow, well, we will just have to hope Sir Arthur does not return before we get the shoes sorted. Now, about the alarm, this house starts early and the clock is in your room for a reason. Make sure you set it from now on."

Nedda pointed to a place at the table and motioned Melody to sit. "This is Lily. She is the day help. She lives in the village and works here five days a week." Lily poured tea in the cup in front of Melody and then passed her the sugar and milk. "I understand you may have some adjustments to make from your trip, at least to do with the differences in time, so today and tomorrow you don't need to start on your work, but if you feel up to it, it's expected."

Melody looked at Nedda, waiting for her to explain the work, but the housekeeper had turned back to the stove to take a plate of toast from the rack. After putting it on the table, Melody started to ask about her duties. "Can you tell me exactly what it is I am expected to do?"

Nedda looked surprised by the question. "Why, you will do whatever Sir Arthur wants you to do. He put some things in the library for you to start on and when he returns, he can tell you more about your duties here. Until then, you can work on what has already been laid out."

Melody put her tea back on the table and turned to Nedda. "Where is my cousin? When will he return?"

Nedda put the last of the food on the table. "It is none of your affair where Sir Arthur is or when he will return. He will be here soon, this is all you need to know. Now, finish your breakfast and I will take you to the library."

The rest of the meal passed in silence. As each person finished, they put their dishes in the sink for washing later. Nedda was mistress of the kitchen and preferred doing them herself. When she and Melody had both finished, Nedda took her to the library.

Melody hadn't seen any section of the house when she arrived except for her quarters, the kitchen, and backstairs. This morning, Nedda led her back down the hall from the kitchen to the foyer where she had come in the night before. The room was large and had several doors and archways leading off from it. One of the archways in the middle of the right side was the entry to a corridor, and at the end of it were two sliding doors which disappeared into the wall on either side of the doorway. They were slightly open, and a room filled with bookcases could be seen beyond.

Nedda opened the two doors fully and walked to the desk that sat near the right side. "This is Sir Arthur's desk. Do not touch anything on it. This little table here is where he wants you to work, and these papers are what you are to start on. If you need anything, don't go looking for it, come to the kitchen and ask me." Before Nedda closed the doors on her way out, she turned and said, "Lunch is at twelve thirty sharp. Don't be late."

Melody looked around. The room was much larger than the library in her home in Houston. All of her family had been avid readers, and each generation added to the books already there. However, the one in her house was dwarfed in size and by the number of volumes which were in this room.

The ceiling was high and the bookcases reached almost to the maximum. A ladder was attached on each wall-to-wall case and ran on rails built into the top. From what she could see, there were no gaping holes, but neither were the books pressed together. It also looked like there was some kind of system which made finding a specific book easy.

The small table Nedda had shown her had several pencils and pens in a cup, a stack of files, and some loose papers. Suddenly, she looked around the room and realized something was missing. There wasn't a computer to be found. She had not brought her laptop with her since she thought her cousin would have one in the house. Perhaps she would find one in another room. However, she remembered the admonition of Nedda and did not go looking to find one.

Judging by the age of the paper, the first few files held letters and notes written over several years. Another had a large family tree that folded out and covered an area much larger than her little table. From what she saw of it, the tree had not been kept up to date and had been left with some holes.

One side of the room had windows that looked out on a park-like setting. A shadow crossed one window and from the corner of her eye, Melody saw movement. Someone was outside and for a split-second, apprehension flashed through her.

A man wearing a long duster and floppy hat knocked on one of the windows. When he raised his head, she saw a pair of sky-blue eyes in a very handsome face. He smiled and motioned for her to raise the window.

Melody looked around, unlatched the window, and raised it. The man removed his hat and smiled at her again. "Hello! You must be Arthur's ward from the United States. I'm his neighbor, Alfred Oswin. And your name?"

"Melody Fitzhugh Farr, Mister Oswin." She extended her hand and sat on the wide window ledge. "Do you know my cousin well?"

Before the man could answer, the door to the study opened and Nedda strode into the room. "Lord Alfred, if you want to see Lord Arthur, he is not here, and before you ask, he has not informed me of when he will return." With a gesture of curt dismissal, she turned to Melody. "Please don't open widows in this or any room. If you need fresh air, the gardens would make a nice place for you to exercise after you have finished your work."

The man made a slow, overly exaggerated courtly bow, wished Melody a fine day, and left across the lawn. Nedda closed and locked the window while Melody resumed her seat at the small desk.

"Nedda, is there a computer I can use for this? I didn't bring mine with me, but this is something which will go much faster with a word processer and a spreadsheet."

The older woman turned back to look at Melody, "Sir Arthur doesn't use such things. What he doesn't write out by hand, he dictates to a secretary. Just get on with doing what you've been asked." Melody watched as the door closed on Nedda.

21

Melody sat at the small table. The first file she opened was full of letters, most written by a feminine hand and addressed to a boy who was at school. The newer letters were in the front and discussed college life, but as she looked further, they regressed to upper and lower grades or forms at a boarding school. The oldest of the posts were particularly poignant because they had been sent to a young boy who had just been sent off to school for the first time, and it was apparent that he was still wracked with homesickness and sadness for being parted from his mother. The undercurrent of those letters showed the mother's sadness at not having her son with her.

Melody supposed the letters were to her cousin from his mother, but it wasn't quite clear. There were few letters in return during the college years, but it looked as if the boys in the boarding school had been tasked with writing to their home at least once a month. Shaky lines, brief sentences, and strikethroughs during the early form years led to just as brief but better penmanship and structure during the latter years. The older the boy became, the less substance there was in each letter.

Melody kept an eye on her watch since she didn't want to further inflame Nedda by being late for lunch. As the time drew near, she closed the dusty file she was working on and left a paper to mark her place. She had a short list of questions for her cousin and laid them aside.

Melody had just left the library and was making her way back down the corridor to the kitchen when she heard a loud crash and shouted words. "Silly girl, look what you've done! Get the mop and clean it up, what is wrong with you?" Nedda's voice carried over the sob of the daygirl, Lily.

When Melody entered the room, the girl was on the floor, cleaning the day's soup from the tiles with sponge and mop and bucket propped against the chair nearest her. The girl looked up at Melody, and she could see the tears that were streaked on Lily's face. Melody made a move to help, but Nedda told her to sit.

"The girl spilled the soup, the girl will clean it up. If you need to wash your hands, the sink in the mud room can be used, but if not, sit so you can eat."

Melody went through the small door Nedda pointed to which led to the mud room. Inside were boots, jackets, and various outside items, as well as a large stone sink. The water was cold but the bar of soap that was on the side helped take the dust from the files off her hands. Clean, she looked around for a towel but didn't see one. As she sat at the table, she used her napkin to dry the excess water.

Nedda's husband, John, came in from the hallway. Lily put the cleaning items away, and Nedda set the rest of the food on the table. Lunch was eaten in silence. Melody thought this would be a good time to ask if John would be going into the village.

"Nedda has pointed out the need for me to have some sensible shoes. There are a few things I didn't bring with me that I would like to buy. If you will be going into the village, I would like to get a ride."

Nedda answered for her husband, "John has work here today. Perhaps tomorrow he will go into the village and you can go then, or, if you want, you can walk, but I don't recommend it in those shoes."

The housekeeper thought the question was behind her, but Melody was quick to ask several follow-ups. "How far is the village? Perhaps I can walk it or even get a taxi to take me. They do have a taxi here, don't they, and a shop where I can get shoes and maybe a mixer hose for the bath?"

Nedda sternly faced Melody to give her an answer, but the doorbell rang and she nodded to her husband who left his unfinished meal to see who would be calling at such an unlikely hour. Sheepishly, he returned to announce the Vicar's wife was calling on Miss Melody Farr.

He handed the lady's card to Melody and expected her to tell him she was "not at home," meaning she wasn't available to visit with the guest. However, Melody put her napkin aside, smoothed her hair, and left for the foyer.

Nedda was beside herself. Who did this American girl think she was, accepting visitors in His Lordship's parlor? Before she could get to the foyer, her husband John was showing the two women into the small day room. She would deal with her husband later.

"I am sorry if I've come at a bad time, but I was just down the road visiting one of the parishioners of my husband's church in the village and Lord Alfred mentioned you'd arrived. My name is Livia Paxton and my husband is the Vicar of St. Alban's Church, the Reverend Charles Paxton." The lady held out her hand and Melody was happy to take it while she introduced herself.

"It is such a pleasure to meet you. I am Melody Fitzhugh Farr, cousin to the owner of this house. Please sit down. I am so happy you came to visit." Seated on adjoining sofas, the women turned when Nedda came in. She didn't look happy, but she was even less so when she saw how cozy the two ladies looked. Icily, she asked Melody, "Would you like some tea? Maybe a bit of cake or fruit?"

Melody found it difficult to understand why Nedda was being so inhospitable, but Livia Paxton sensed the problem. "Oh please, nothing for me, I have just come from a bit of tea and cake at the last house I visited. This is just some unplanned visiting and I won't be long."

Nedda retreated from the room with a loud "humph" to accent her departure.

Livia turned to the American girl. She was not the plain Jane one would expect under the circumstances. People in the district had heard Lord Arthur would be ward to an unmarried American cousin in her late twenties, but it was assumed she was both poor and surely not very good-looking if she hadn't been able to find a husband. Melody was really a rather striking young girl. She walked well, her voice reflected her name, and she seemed to be poised, if a little out of her natural element. Few Americans would be comfortable in this kind of situation, so this could be a part of her mild discomfort.

Melody was pleased to have Nedda out of the room. "Please tell me, what time are services on Sundays? My family members in Houston were always regular church goers and even at university, I attended most Sunday mornings."

"On Sundays we have service at nine and every Wednesday evening at six we have Evening Prayer. It isn't a large congregation, but we do keep active. Perhaps my husband and I can call on you at a more appropriate time?"

"Oh, please do, I would enjoy it and you can expect to see me at services on Sunday. Can you tell me some things about the village?

I was asking Nedda, but she isn't inclined to say much. Is there a taxi service? Do they have shops where I can get some 'sensible shoes,' perhaps a mixer hose for the bath, those kinds of things?"

"There is a taxi service and there are some shops, but why don't I take you? I have finished my visiting for the day and Charles won't be expecting me for another hour or so. Get your things then and let's go!"

Melody smiled and as she was saying, "Thank you," she was heading out the door. Nedda was in the foyer area, probably waiting for the Vicar's wife to leave, and Melody told her she would be going with Livia to the village. "I just need to get my purse and jacket."

Nedda was fuming as she watched Melody head up the main staircase. She had not been given permission to use any part of the main house except the library. She didn't know what to do with the girl.

Before Sir Arthur left, he had given her the letter he had written to the bank in Houston and told her to send a list of things Melody would need when she got to Farr Cottage. She had done as instructed, but the stupid girl didn't even know what sensible shoes meant, clacking around in heels like she did. He had laid out the things he wanted her to start on and said he would be back.

Livia Paxton waited in the foyer and watched Nedda. Forty some years at being a Vicar's wife meant a lot of contact with people in all sorts of moods, and she could tell Nedda was not happy. Melody seemed like a nice girl, she dressed a little somber for a girl her age, but she had just lost her mother and she may just not want to wear bright colors so soon. She turned when she heard the girl's step on the stairs.

"Oh, you may want to bring an umbrella with you. It can rain anytime here, and it would be silly to be caught without one." Livia turned to Nedda. "I will have her back in a couple of hours. What time is her tea?"

Barely able to contain her rage, Nedda told both women she would serve the tea at four thirty "sharp!" She turned on her heel and headed through the door to the kitchen.

"I need to buy an umbrella then, don't I?" Melody said as she followed Livia to her car.

The trip to the village with the Vicar's wife gave Melody a chance to see the outside of Farr Cottage in the daytime. It was a very large house, not what would really be called a "cottage" where she was from. She had looked at the stone and brick building as the car backed around and headed down the drive. Ivy covered a large portion of the structure and the third floor where her room was located, not the top floor, but the last might have been attics.

The grounds were large and modestly well-kept, but the hedges needed some trimming and she reminded herself she wanted to see if there were any gardens. In school she had read descriptions of some of the great English or Italian gardens in Britain and wondered if the house even had one. Nedda didn't mention a gardener, and if her husband, John, was responsible for them, he must need help to let the hedges go so badly.

The village shops were not department stores, but with visits to three different ones, she was able to find the things she wanted. The second to the last place she went was the post office, to buy a cell phone. She didn't want a fancy one, but she would need some overseas minutes to keep in touch with the trustees.

The first thing she needed them to do was ship her the laptop she had left with a friend. Melody asked Livia about internet service and with a laugh, Livia told her, her grandson Peter was the one to talk to about anything to do with computers. Peter had a small shop down the road from the green-grocers and was the last place they went.

Peter was a quiet young man who had been into computers since he was old enough to sit. His father had been a middle management employee of an American company and had most every electronic gadget on the market. Peter had attended a polytechnic after he finished high school, and the shop he ran had just started paying his bills.

He kissed his grandmother and shook Melody's hand. "I can help with the Internet. Britain is going Wi-Fi in an attempt to give everyone access to the Internet. The Cottage should have no problem picking up a signal. If you want, I can let you use a laptop until yours gets here. I use an encryption program on my equipment to make sure hackers can't get into my stuff, and when you get your machine, I'll fix it so it's safe too."

Melody accepted the help and asked Livia to tell her where to find the taxi. Before she could answer, Peter offered to take her home.

"I was about to close for the afternoon anyway. There is a network problem at the new hotel on the other side of the village, and you wouldn't be too much out of the way. Let me take you." Livia nodded to her and Melody accepted.

Peter had a three-wheeled delivery-type van, and he put Melody's purchases in the back. The interior was clean and well-organized, making it look roomier than it was.

Melody thanked him as he left her in front of the main door of the Cottage.

Before Melody could ring the bell, the door opened and Nedda was standing in the way. "So did you get everything you wanted then? I hope so, you can work tonight to make up for the time you were gone. Tea will be at four thirty, don't be late."

Melody took her packages and instead of putting them in her room, took them to the library so she could get to work. She wanted to make up for any time Nedda thought was owed, although she had thought today and tomorrow were days she would not be expected to do any work.

Before she started, she plugged in the laptop and allowed it to go through the start-up. Just as Peter had said, the Internet popped up with no problem. She had an e-mail address and although she had told everyone—well, the few people she knew—that she would not be online for a while, she checked to see if there were any messages. Mostly all she had were advertisements and spam, but one person she had not had a chance to tell of her impending travels had sent her a short note. Melody answered her and started her work on the files.

As the time neared four thirty, she closed the files, took her packages and the laptop. This time she used the back staircase through the kitchen. Nedda was nowhere to be seen, but the girl Lily was at the sink filling the big kettle. Melody put her things away, plugged the laptop into the lone plug in her room, and washed for tea. She also put on the shoes she had bought in the village.

The shoes were black leather with a rubber sole which made no noise. They were not unlike the shoes she had worn with her school uniform when she went to the Anglican high school in Houston. She had also purchased some cotton socks to wear with them and polish to keep them nice. If she was going to try walking into the village, she would wear these shoes and carry her heels with her. It might make for a bulky purse or bag, but it would be fine once she got used to doing it this way.

Precisely at four thirty, she sat at the kitchen table for tea. The servants in the house still had "tea" instead of supper or dinner, and although Melody wasn't used to eating her evening meal so early, she didn't object. Except for requests for salt, and the passing of items from the other end of the table, nothing was said during the meal. Lily stayed to help clear up and then got on her bicycle to go home. Melody returned to work in the library.

It was after eight in the evening before she felt she had done a full day's work and turned out the lights. She still hadn't seen any other sections of the house other than the kitchen, back stairs, and a brief walk down the main corridor past closed rooms. The outside was also a new place for her to explore.

Before leaving the library, she had looked out the windows onto the parkland. A light rain was falling, and any hope of taking a walk was out of the question. She would do it in the coming days. It bothered her when she was not offered a tour of the home where she might live for the next few years. Nothing had been said by the trustees, the lawyer, or in her cousin's letter, but she didn't know how long she should expect to be at the Cottage.

Melody washed her hair using the mixer hose she purchased at the shop and dried it as best she could with a towel. She was going to be up some time yet doing some Internet research so there should be plenty of time for it to dry. A solution for her clothes was still a priority, but she would wait until Nedda was in a better mood before asking. More than an hour into her Internet search, she heard Nedda's shoes on the bare wood floors. She knocked on the door then entered. "What are you doing up so late? You should be in bed. Set your alarm and turn off the machine. No one gave you permission to have it here. On second thought, give it to me and I'll get rid of it."

Melody put her hands on the machine. "It's not mine. Peter, the grandson of the Vicar's wife, let me use it. I'll turn it off, but you can't have it."

Nedda backed away. "All right, but set the alarm and go to sleep." Without even a "good night," she left.

Melody checked her hair and found it almost dry. It would have to do. She had looked in a local shop for a hairdryer when she was in the village and now wished she had gotten one.

<hr/>

The alarm was really loud and it gave Melody a start when she realized where she was. Each morning she said morning prayers just as she said her evening prayers before bed. Dressed and ready, she got to the kitchen a few minutes before breakfast.

Lily looked at her feet and saw the leather oxfords Melody was wearing and then smiled but didn't say anything. It struck Melody much of the day in this house was spent in silence. No one talked unless they needed to, and this included during meals. She was anxious to get back to the work in the library.

The days moved along into another until late on Friday morning when a delivery truck stopped at the front door. The driver, a young man of no more than twenty, pulled a package from the back of the truck and rang the bell. Nedda answered the door and her raised voice could be heard through the closed door of the library.

"Don't you know deliveries come to the back?" A short pause meant the delivery man was answering or asking her something before she continued. "No, boy, I will sign for it—oh well, if you insist." Melody heard Nedda come down the hall.

A knock on the door and Nedda came in. "There is a package for you, and the delivery boy insists you have to be the one to sign."

Before Melody could answer, Nedda was gone and she was left standing by the young man in the foyer with the large package. He set it down and handed a clipboard and pen to Melody. She signed her name, took the box, and went back to the library. Nedda followed.

When Nedda opened the door to the library, the box sat on the floor and Melody had resumed her work. When Melody looked up, she offered, "It's some personal things I had sent to me from home. I'll open it later in my room." Nedda started to say something but turned and left.

In the evening, in her room, she opened a box which was too big to have only a laptop in it. Her machine was there with a great deal of packing. The people who sent it must have been worried it would not travel safely. There was also a shipping bill enclosed which detailed the money used to get the computer from her friend's safe keeping, packed, and shipped to her. The fees charged by the trustees for "client services" were a bit more than she had anticipated. It made her think this was the last time she would ask them to do anything without querying the price first.

The next day she took both of the laptops, hers and Peter's, to his shop. She thanked him for the use of the machine, and he put the encryption program on her machine so she could use the Wi-Fi without problems. She also stopped at the shop where she had seen the hairdryer and purchased it. In a corner of the next shop she entered were a stack of thick, warm blankets, and she thought it might be a good idea to get at least one if not two. It was still summer, her room was already cold, and she worried it would be worse in winter. Melody paid for two blankets and a set of soft cotton sheets.

She'd told Nedda she would not be home for lunch but would eat in the village. It was almost one before she entered the pub's public room and took a seat in a corner booth to order a sandwich. The bench seat across from her was filled with the purchases and her laptop.

The food was good, but before she could finish, Lord Alfred came in and saw her sitting by herself. He asked if he might join her and before she could answer, he'd pulled up a chair and sat down.

"So, Miss Melody, how are you enjoying your stay at Farr Cottage? You must be terribly busy if you can't return my calls or at least leave me a message." There was a strong note of disapproval in his voice. "I was hoping to give you a tour of the area, if your work will allow."

Melody was puzzled. This was the first she had heard of messages or calls. "I don't know what you're talking about. There have been no calls or messages. The library doesn't have a phone, but I have a private cell phone. Do you want my number?"

While she pulled her phone from her purse, she had a suspicion the problem was not the phone system but the persons or person taking the messages. Nedda would have this under her control, and Melody hadn't gotten any messages or notes from her.

Lord Alfred's face broke into a smile. "Hmm. I think it must be Nedda. She answered every time I called and it was always the same. 'You are busy working, but she would give you the message.' Doesn't look like she remembers messages very well. If you are willing to give me your number, I would appreciate the trust."

Melody wrote the number on a slip of paper and he put it in his phone. "There, now if I want to talk to you, to, say, invite you to dinner, all I have to do is push this button."

Her phone started to vibrate in her hand. She cancelled the call and put the number in under a listing for L. Alfred. "I have to get these things back to the house. Livia Paxton gave me the number for the taxi service, but I wasn't going to call until I finished lunch."

Alfred looked at the pile of things and realized it was mostly bedding. "Are you finding the old place a bit cold? You have some serious winter blankets in this pile. Are they short on featherbeds and bedcovers?"

"In my room, or at least the one they put me in, it is very cold. No heater, a couple of very thin blankets and very rough cotton sheets. When I return to my home in Houston, these will work just fine in one of the small guest rooms."

Alfred was beginning to get the impression Nedda was treating Melody more like a servant or employee of Lord Arthur than his guest and ward. Arthur had left so suddenly after agreeing to be her guardian; Alfred was convinced he had left the details up to his housekeeper. "Tell me, do you eat by yourself in the big dining room, smaller breakfast room, or in the kitchen with the staff?"

Melody laid her sandwich down. "I eat in the kitchen, my room is on the third floor, and the facilities are down the hall. I recognize servant's quarters when I see them. My home in Houston used to have a full staff when my grandmother was alive, but no more. Until my cousin arrives, it will stay the way it is and if this is his wish, for me to stay in the servant's hall, then I think my visit will be quite short." She dabbed her mouth with the napkin and pushed her plate away. "I may be an American, but my family was well-off both socially as well as financially. I attended some fine private schools and an equally impressive private university where I received a master's degree in History. So you see, I do know the difference between 'guest' and 'employee/servant'."

The barmaid who had served her food came to the table. Melody handed her a few pound notes and picked up her purse to leave. Alfred put his hand over hers. "Please don't leave. I still want to invite you to dinner and now I have you here, it would be nice to have a chance to talk to you more. What about tonight?"

Melody settled back into the booth. "I would like to take you up on the dinner invitation, but not this evening. Now my laptop is here and I can use the Internet, there are some things which need my attention, like getting my regular clothes here."

Alfred was not going to give up so quickly. "Lunch tomorrow then? I can get you about eleven and take you to a restaurant near the river."

She shook her head. "Tomorrow I will probably not be out of church before eleven. Now, really I must go. I still have to call the taxi."

In a final plea for her to stay, Alfred offered to take her home and pick her up for church the next morning. "I would be happy to escort you to church. In fact, it has been a while since I've been there, and I'm sure the Vicar will like having me in the audience. After church, we can have lunch, but let me take you back to the Cottage."

Melody would have given in to his entreaties, but she had some shopping yet to do. "Yes, I will accept your invitation to church and lunch, but there is something I need to do yet here in the village.

Hmm…" She looked at her packages. "I suppose the shop will have to send these with the rest of the things they sold me today."

Alfred was out of his seat and was picking up the parcels before Melody could object. "I will put these in my car. You can finish your shopping, and all you have to do is call and I will be there in minutes to take you to the Cottage." He winked. "Faster than the taxi, I promise."

Finally, she gave in to his suggestions. "I will keep my laptop with me, but all right, take these and it should only take me a few minutes in the ladies' clothing store down on the High Street."

He chuckled. "I will expect you when you're finished. My mother and grandmother used to tell me a 'few minutes' and it was always longer. When you're done, just call." Alfred put her things in the back of an old Range Rover in the parking lot and walked to one of the outside tables at the pub to wait.

The ladies' shop was small and mid-priced. Melody had passed it a couple of times but hadn't ever stopped. There were flowered dresses, skirts, and sweater sets, and in the back, a few summer hats, gloves, and purses. It only took her a few minutes to pull a dress, two twinsets to go with her black skirts, and a hat, glove, and purse ensemble for church. Alfred saw Melody leave the shop with the packages and he pulled the car up in front to put her packages in the trunk. "When you said a few minutes, you don't give a guy time to even finish a half-pint." Hmm. A girl of her word, fascinating.

Lord Alfred helped her with her packages as far as the foyer. Nedda looked on in displeasure, but told her husband to take them to Melody's room. Before he left, Alfred made a point of telling Melody what time he would pick her up in the morning for church.

Melody spent the remainder of the afternoon in her room. The dress she had bought at the store fit perfectly, even the length was good, and it went well with the hat she had gotten. She put one of the twinsets on, a light blue one, and it helped keep her warm. With the new sheets on the bed and the blankets piled high, the night would not feel as cold.

At the place she had gotten the mixer hose, she had also bought a spray can of lubricant and the bedsprings and frame got a good helping to relieve the screeching they made when Melody was trying to sleep. Except for not having a place to hang her clothes, the room was almost livable.

Melody had one good friend in Houston; the girl who had kept her laptop for her was a pal from college. She caught her online and asked her to get some of her things from the house. Melody had left a key with her and knew she could trust her. By the time the two girls had signed off, Melody's friend had a long list of clothes and shoes she would box and send to Farr Cottage at the beginning of the week.

———————

Sunday morning was sunny and warm. Melody never ate breakfast on a day when she would take Communion, and this Sunday was no different. She had told Nedda the day before not to expect her for breakfast, so the first time she saw her was when Lord Alfred came to get her for church. The flowered mid-calf dress fit her willowy figure very well, and her curves showed even better when a breeze blew the fabric against her body. Melody had a good sized bust line, curvy hips, long legs, and slender ankles. The high heels she wore made her normal five-foot-seven more like five- nine or -ten. While most women had quit wearing hats, the one she had bought from the local shop framed her face nicely and her thick chestnut-brown colored hair flowed from underneath. Melody was a striking young lady!

Lord Alfred was impressed. He had looked her over quite well when he had called the first day and again the day before in the pub, but he hadn't seen her like this. She wasn't what he or anyone had expected. Although the first day had quieted the idea that she was unmarried because she was ugly or plain, no one could've guessed she looked this good. He parked in the church lot, opened her door, and escorted her into the sanctuary. The congregation was small and because it was summer, many people were on holiday, and the attendance was meager. The Farr's had a pew in the front and on the other side of the aisle, another pew, long unused, was for his family, the Oswins. Today he chose to sit with Melody in the Farr pew and hoped it wouldn't upset the ghosts of long-dead Farr ancestors.

The Reverend Charles Paxton was pleased to see the American girl his wife had told him about in the Farr pew, but he was stunned when he recognized Lord Alfred Oswin sitting beside her. It had been years since the man had been in church for anything besides a wedding or funeral, and he wondered what had brought him this Sunday. As he stood in the pulpit to give the sermon, he saw the girl in the front pew looking up at him and understood what had brought the Oswin boy to church.

It hit him halfway through his sermon that the pew Lord Alfred was sitting in was the Farr pew and hoped no one else understood what it meant. This parish was full of gossips, so word would get back to Lord Arthur when he returned, but at least the Oswin boy was in church. The pew problem could be sorted out later.

Reverend Paxton, with his wife Livia standing next to him, greeted each parishioner as he or she left after the service. When the American girl approached, the Reverend's wife introduced her. "Charles, this is Melody Farr, ward of Lord Arthur Farr. I met Melody when she first arrived."

Charles Paxton enthusiastically shook the young lady's hand and, seeing her up close up, was struck by her beauty. He could see why young Oswin was so attentive. "I am so happy to see you in church. Mrs. Paxton told me you were a regular attendee at your church in Houston, Texas. I hope you will be in our church regularly while you are here."

Melody smiled at him and his wife. "My family has been members of my church at home since my great-great grandfather helped establish it when he immigrated to Texas in the 1800s. There has been a Farr on the Vestry there since its founding…well, at least until my mother died a couple of months ago. And I will be here every Sunday, if possible, and I'll try to make the Wednesday services too."

As she stepped forward, Lord Alfred shook the Vicar's hand and thought he could pass without having to engage him in conversation, but Reverend Paxton would have none of it. "Lord Alfred, how nice of you to come! The last time I saw you at a service that wasn't a funeral or a wedding, you were in short trousers. Can I credit Miss Farr for getting you to come?"

Alfred cleared his throat. "Well I am taking her to lunch and she wouldn't go until after church, so it made sense to come, but we must be leaving. Nice sermon." Alfred took Melody's arm and steered her toward the Rover as the Vicar and his wife looked after them.

———— ⋅《◉》⋅ ————

The restaurant Alfred had chosen was part of an old, traditional hotel. The building sat on the road but backed up to a river with boats going by. The rear wall was glass, and a large patio accommodated several tables for those wanting to eat outside in fine weather. Alfred asked for a table next to the windows, but inside. It just wouldn't do to have to stop their meal because of rain.

The meeting in the pub had been accidental, but Lord Alfred taking Melody to church and then to lunch was something else. It was fodder for the local gossip and before the first course was put on the table, most people in the district knew about their lunch.

Alfred and Melody were mostly unaware of the talk they were creating: Melody because she didn't know she could be news; and Alfred because he just didn't care. He had been the subject of a lot of gossip in his day and it didn't worry him. For most of the people, regular life was a little boring, and this gave them something to discuss.

———— ⋅《◉》⋅ ————

No one knew the American girl, but everyone knew Lord Alfred. The only son of Sir Alden Alfred Oswin and Lady Mayda Elizabeth Firzwilliam, he had been a hellion since he was a child. His father's answer to his naughtiness was to send him to public school, and his mother was just happy to have him out of the house. The father did something in the city and the mother enjoyed the endless parties that living in London made available to them both.

Although the first few years of public school didn't agree with him, one very stern headmaster was finally able to get Alfred to understand the world didn't revolve around him and it certainly didn't owe him anything. His grades came up and were at least good enough to get him into Oxford. The change in attitude surprised his parents, and his father was especially pleased. He wanted his boy to be more than a wastrel. The Oswin family was old and could trace their name and tree back to the Anglo-Saxons who had fought the invasion by the bastard Duke of Normandy. Unlike many old English families, they were known less for having only a few scoundrels or dilatants, but actually for being boring, sober members of society. Like the Farrs, money and land was saved and invested, not wasted on drink, riotous living, gambling, or lose women.

The second year Alfred was in Oxford his father invited him to go skiing with him and his mother. Alfred had a serious paper due and asked to be excused. The small jet his parents were in crashed in the Alps during a storm and both perished. Alfred left university and returned to the family home. He was barely twenty-two.

The Oswin family had a house in London where the couple had lived most of the year, but there was also the old family estate not too distant from Farr Cottage. When Alfred had told Melody he was a close neighbor, he realized he was one with respect to proximity, nothing more. The London house was what made him a close neighbor.

The estate, Aldwin, was not used much, and it hadn't had steady occupants since his grandmother died when he was eleven. He remembered being allowed to come home for her funeral, but then had to be back at school before bed check at nine o'clock. His mother had inquired to make sure he understood what "dead" meant and if he was all right, but then left him sitting on a couch the rest of the time he was there. Alfred had a chance—actually, it was his only chance—to watch his mother and father in a social setting. He had never been allowed to attend any of their parties and was usually sent somewhere with his nanny or a servant when he was not in school. His mother flitted from one group of people to another and his father stayed with the men in the study. Neither one paid him any attention, and he didn't miss it. He was anxious to be back at school among friends. Then they died, the funeral was held at the local church, the one he had attended this morning with Melody. His parents were buried in the family crypt. The wake was held in the same old house as his grandmother's. After the double funeral, he closed Aldwin and went to live in the house in London.

Lord Alfred inherited the title, the land, everything, because he was the last of his line—well, almost the last. Modern DNA testing could have cleared many things, but the stubborn man who was Melody's guardian wouldn't hear of having the test done. They both knew they were cousins, but Lord Arthur would never admit to the truth. Alfred was hoping the genealogy work Melody would be doing would prove the connection.

Melody was enjoying her lunch. She had heard the food in England was overcooked, tasteless, and pedestrian, but her fish was well-prepared and flavorful. She was, however, more interested in her dinner companion than the food.

She was tall, especially in heels, but Alfred was able to tower over her. At well over six feet, he made her look a normal height. He was well-muscled, looked athletic, and had a light caramel-colored head of hair to go with the sky- blue eyes she had noticed the first day.

During lunch, they talked about several things: her life in Houston, the years she was in university, and computers. Alfred had a computer, but for him it was just another tool, not something he was really into, like Melody. He told her some of the things he had studied at Oxford, but stopped short of telling her the reason he left there so suddenly.

It was when they got to dessert she asked him what he did for a living. He didn't want to tell her exactly what he did, but there was really no shame in not working. He simply managed what he had inherited and lived off the income.

"So you don't really have a job you go to, you just do this from home?" she asked between bites. "What about your father's business, didn't you want to follow in his footsteps?" Alfred laid his fork on the plate. "My father dealt in *influence*. If someone wanted something done by parliament or a government department, he would know the right person to talk to or the best group to try to sway to get things done. People would pay him a fee for his help. I was never a part of their world and didn't have the kind of contacts needed to keep it going. No, this is one case of a son not following his father into the business. There was no *and Son* to go on my father's sign.

"I live most of the time in London, but only part of the house is even used. I've been thinking about selling up and coming back to the country for good, but Aldwin needs some work also. It's just a matter of which one means more to me." The waitress came to pour more coffee and then Alfred continued, "Aldwin has been in the family since before the Normans invaded. One of the bastard's knights took it and he married the daughter of the house. The marriage never produced an heir, but a cousin of hers, Rand Oswin, was adopted by them as a young boy and he inherited. This is the why the Oswin name remained with the estate."

Melody had more questions, but lunch was over and she felt it was enough information for one day. She liked Alfred's company, but everything was so new to her, she was cautious.

—————⊙—————

She had never had many dates. Any spare time at university was taken up with study or visiting her ailing mother at home. Her high school years were spent in a private girl's school, so male companionship was hard to come by. The only place she ever met anyone was at church or the country club.

Her mother had insisted on dancing lessons and at one time wanted her to have a "coming out" party, but it was a practice which was not really the fashion—and in Houston, even less so. Friends of her mother would arrange for her to go out with their sons, with her mother's blessings of course, but such arranged occasions were usually only one- time events. At twenty-eight, she had never had a serious relationship, nothing even close, and she was wary of getting into one.

Alfred had promised her a drive in the country, but it started to rain as they left the restaurant. By the time he got out onto the road, it was a downpour. "I hate this," he said, "but perhaps we can do the drive another day. You won't be able to see a thing in this rain."

Melody agreed and he headed to the Cottage. As he pulled up to the front door, the rain was still coming down hard. He idled the motor and they waited for the rain to let up a bit. After ten minutes, the storm started to abate, but the front door opened and John, holding a large umbrella, came to open her door.

Melody was fairly dry when she got inside, but Alfred wasn't. She offered to get him a towel to dry off and left to fetch one from the kitchen. Part way back down the hall, she heard the raised voices. Towel in hand, Melody got back to the foyer in time to see Alfred and the man who must be her guardian having "words" by the front door.

The older of the two men was working to keep his voice calm despite his obvious agitation. "You have no reason to be in my house, now I ask you to please leave."

John stood with the front door open, but Alfred wasn't budging. "I am here to bring Melody home. We just finished lunch."

"It was very big of you to take her, but she doesn't need your company. In the future, call me if you wish to see her."

"And leave a message with Nedda? Right, I left messages with her and not one was delivered. I have as much right to see Melody as anyone." He turned and accepted the towel from her. All but ignoring Arthur. "Would you like me to take you Wednesday?"

Before he finished, Arthur interjected, "I will take my ward where she wants to go on Wednesday or any other day."

Alfred grinned. "Then you will be the one to take her to church on Wednesday evening? Oh, I have to see this. Vicar Paxton was apoplectic when I took her this morning, I can't wait to see what he will do if he sees both of us there."

Arthur balked. "Well, uh, yes, I will take her. Now, your business is done here so go." He turned away from Alfred dismissively and addressed Melody for the first time. "I am your guardian and right now. I think it is best if you go to your room before dinner."

It was too much for Alfred. "Melody, please tell Lord Arthur where his ward's room is located and how you have been treated since you arrived. He may want to look at his own house and employees before he starts throwing innocent neighbors out."

Arthur turned on Alfred and he was fuming. In a quiet, strong voice, he told John, "Please escort His Lordship from the house."

As Alfred left, he heard Arthur bellow, "Nedda! Nedda!" As much as Alfred would have loved to see what happened to the housekeeper, he still had Melody's cell number and knew he could call her when he wanted. He'd known Arthur could return at any time, but he had hoped to have more time to get to know the girl before her guardian came back to put roadblocks in his way. Nevertheless, he did feel good about the progress he had made with her and smiled as he turned the car around in the driveway.

Melody was waiting in the library while Nedda and her guardian talked in the lounge. She hadn't wanted anyone to say anything to him about her living conditions—at least not yet—but she supposed Alfred had used it as a defense for taking an interest in her.

As she heard Nedda retreat from the lounge, the door to the library opened. It was the first time she really had a chance to take a good look at her guardian and she guessed it was the same for him. He was about the same height as Alfred and the two men were of equal build and weight. The hair color was not too different, but Lord Arthur did have some grey at his temples. She guessed he was at least ten years older than Alfred was, but she had never been good at guessing ages. The picture, which had been included with the letter, looked like him, but did not resemble him entirely. To her eyes, the two men were very similar, but then she hadn't had time to see much of either man. While she eyed him, her cousin was looking her over.

He had been worried his cousin would be an awkward, ugly, or plain young woman. What he saw before him was a willowy but curvy young lady with a mass of chestnut- brown hair, dark eyes, and a handsome face. She was tall, and the heels she was wearing made her even taller. She walked with ease and didn't shy away from the unpleasant exchange which she had just witnessed in the hall.

He put his hand out to her. "I suppose we can start over with the formal introductions. I am your cousin, Albert Farr, and I am sorry I was not here when you arrived. Business matters made it impossible. Please sit down. Let me apologize for Nedda, it seems she didn't quite understand what your place was to be here in the house. As we speak, your things are being moved to a nice room on the second floor, which you should find much more comfortable."

Melody took the offered hand, shook it, and sat down. "Thank you, cousin. I had guessed as much, but no harm has been done, except it would be nice to receive my messages in the future."

"Melody, the relationship I have with Lord Alfred is compli-cated. He knows he is not welcome in this house and he should never have approached you without my permission. Just leave it and trust me when I tell you he is not right for you."

"Lord Albert, I was happy Alfred took me to church and lunch, but it does not constitute a 'relationship' where I come from, so don't worry over it. I also think, barring father's will, I am of an age to decide with whom I shall be friends. However, I am in your house and will abide by your wishes."

"Thank you. We dress for dinner here and eat at six thirty. Before the meal, I have a cocktail in the lounge. I invite you to join me at five thirty. So, if there is nothing else, I have work to do." He turned in dismissal, but before he left the room, he said over his shoulder, "Have a nice afternoon."

She sat looking after him. *Hmm, so this is my "guardian"?* Melody shook her head and went off to find her room and put her things away.

She spent the rest of the afternoon settling in. Her room was large, had a couple of big windows, which looked out over the park, and was blue, her favorite color. Nedda had moved her belongings and put them away, but Melody had her own way of putting her things in drawers, and—now that she had a closet—of putting her clothes on the hangers. There was a wooden writing desk between the two windows where she could put her laptop. However, the item she liked the most was the attached bathroom and toilet.

She still needed the mixer hose she had bought, but the tub was newer—well, newer than the one she had been using. It was big and long enough for her to stretch out. It was so relaxing!

Melody expected her clothes to arrive from America in the next few days or so, but she needed to wear something to dinner. She went down to the kitchen and found Nedda making the soup. When Melody started to talk to her, Nedda's behavior was very different from her manners in the days since she had arrived.

"Yes, miss, I think we might have something you could wear. I will bring it to your room in a few minutes."

Melody thanked her and went back upstairs. She was happy she had brought the two pair of black heels—at least she would have proper shoes to go with whatever Nedda brought her.

The dress Nedda produced was a little big for Melody's frame, but the length was fine with the heels. A belt helped to shape it to her, and she spent some time doing her hair. Rarely did she wear makeup, and it was not something she had brought.

At six o'clock, she walked into the lounge and found her cousin standing by the window, looking out over the lawn. He turned when he heard her heels on the polished wood floor. "You look very nice. Do I recognize the dress?"

"You might, my clothes will not be here until this week some time, and Nedda found this for me to wear. It's a bit big, but the belt helps some. I'm just glad she found it for me."

"Well, since she was the one to write the silly list of things for you to bring, she should find you something. I'm just glad you could use it. I think it was one of my mother's favorite dresses."

"Oh, I'm sorry. I didn't know it might have meant something special to you. From now on, I'll ask you first." Melody blushed slightly and Arthur saw her discomfort.

This girl was deeper than he'd expected. What little contact he'd had with women were his mother and one failed relationship when he was in university. His mother had been a serial shopper and so was the girl at school. This one might be cut from different cloth.

"Don't worry. At least we had something here for you. Now, what can I get you to drink? I've some wine, brandy, whiskey, uh, what you probably call scotch, just take your pick."

"I'll have the whiskey please," Melody said as she sat on the little ladies chair Arthur's mother had always used when she and his father had been in residence at the Cottage.

Arthur made her the drink and they sat talking until John called them to dinner. The dining room was next to the lounge and could seat at least twelve comfortably. The library in this house was bigger than the one in her home in Houston, but the dining room was smaller.

When her great-grandfather built the additions onto the house originally built by his father, he was a successful banker with a socialite wife. They did a considerable amount of entertaining and it showed in the large dining room, living rooms, and patios. Her grandmother used to tell her stories about some of the parties she had seen her parents-in-law give.

During dinner, Arthur made a point of watching how Melody behaved. He hadn't expected her to have the kind of manners his people learned from birth, but he couldn't see any flaws.

They talked a little during dinner, but the subjects were light and had little to do with either the work he had mentioned in his letter, her background, or anything more about Lord Arthur. He offered her a brandy after dinner, but she declined and wished him a good night.

Melody spent some of the time before bed chatting with her friend on the computer. The time difference was a little hard to adjust. Both friends were able to catch up on the news and her friend wanted to know her impression of her cousin and where she was staying.

Breakfast the next morning was served in a small breakfast room with windows to let in the sun and with a view of the gardens. Melody could see the condition of the gardens was not very good, and it would take considerable work to get them back to what they should be. She asked her cousin about them, but he only shrugged and changed the subject.

This would be the first morning she would be working in the library with her cousin, and she hoped he would tell her more about what it was he wanted her to do. She brought in her laptop, set it up, and waited for him to begin.

The computer was the first discordant thing for them to discuss.

"Must you have this thing in here? Don't you know how to type on a regular typewriter?" The look on her cousin's face reminded her of a child finding a scary bug. "I don't like or use them."

"Lord Arthur, this is my laptop, and for the things I have been doing while you are gone, it has worked well. I do know how to type, all of my papers and theses were done on this machine or the one I had before it. It would be silly to reject the use of technology because you are unfamiliar with it. And I am not a secretary but a university-trained historian." She had worked hard to get her degrees, and her cousin needed to respect her abilities.

"Humph, if you insist, but keep it away from me." He sat down at his desk to start work.

"Cousin, I will make sure it doesn't bite you." Melody smiled to herself. She had encountered some people who didn't like computers because they were unfamiliar, but not one of them was as bad as Arthur.

Just as sweetly as can be, she stood by his desk and asked him, "What is it you would like for me to do? I have gone through the files you left on my desk, but the family tree is missing some information. Is that the next thing you want?" He looked up and was a bit bothered at the interruption. "The family tree can wait. I want these files catalogued, and the letters put in their proper place in the filing cabinet." He showed her where to find what he was talking about and expected her to get back to work.

Very quickly, Melody became engrossed in what she was doing. The letters in the files he handed her had vaguely familiar names and dates. Soon she realized why. When she was in high school, a teacher of hers had assigned each of the students the task of doing a genealogy. While it wasn't anything fancy or detailed, hers had been one of the better ones. Everyone in her home knew the family history and had been eager to help.

She was reading letters her great-great grandfather had written back to England when he had immigrated to Texas in the 1870s. She looked through the file. There weren't many letters, but the ones which were there were some she had never seen before.

Melody settled down to read her family's story.

The New World of
Farr Cottage

Late 1870s

R ichard Arthur Farr looked over the rail of the steamship
as it docked at the port of Houston, Texas. It was a small
but busy place; not nearly the size of the one he left in
Portsmouth, England, but for such a young city, it would be ade-
quate for the present. The porter took Richard's bags from his room
and when the cargo hold was emptied, his trunk would be brought
to him.

Richard had become acquainted with two other gentlemen on
the long voyage over. Both had family in Texas and were anxious to
get on with their trip. Some of the other passengers would stay for
a night or two in Houston before moving along, but Richard was
looking forward to getting to his destination.

Until now, however, he wasn't quite sure exactly where this destination would be. He was the fourth son of the fifteenth Viscount
of Gibbons but, with three older brothers, had no hope of inheriting.
The first son, by law, in his family always became the next Viscount,
the second took a commission in the military, and the third went
into the church. Plans didn't usually extend to the odd chance of
having a fourth son.

It was unusual for it to happen, but in Richard's case, he was sent up to Oxford while his next older brother was there studying theology. He had a knack for numbers and when he took his degree, a group of gentlemen saw promise in him and sent him to the city to study banking. When these same men invested their money in the American west, they trusted him to travel to Texas and watch over their investments.

Most of the men had no idea what Texas was like, the scale on which cattle ranching was conducted, or how dangerous such enterprises were. A freak storm in spring or early fall could freeze the livestock in the pastures. While a cow and calf unit in England needed only one acre to thrive, in the American west it could range up to twenty-five acres. These were all things Richard would have to learn for himself. The Cattleman's Hotel was just the place for him to stay while he conducted the group's business. He was to meet a Mr. John Chadwick at the end of the week and travel to the Chadwick Ranch from Houston. In the interim, he wanted a chance to walk around and become acquainted with where he planned on living for the next few years.

Richard was not a small man. At well over six feet tall, he was above average in height but tended to the slim side. A shock of light brown hair and icy-blue eyes gave him a handsome face but not so handsome as to be called pretty. Having three older brothers to compete with in games had kept him in good shape athletically, but in brains, he beat them far and away.

While working in the city of London, he had taken advantage of access to top quality tailors, boot makers, and haberdashers who supplied the gloves, hats, and other odds and ends a young gentleman used. He wore his clothes, unlike some young men who allowed the clothes to wear them. His tall, slim frame made whatever he wore look good. Richard also carried a valuable family trait with him: stability. While many families had suffered from sons who were profligates, down through the generations of Farrs there were no drunkards, gamblers, free-spenders, or fornicators. They were simply a family, which served their king or queen when asked, kept quietly in the country when not occupied elsewhere, and as viewed from the outside, were quite dull. Through the years, some of the young men distinguished themselves militarily and more than one became a bishop. None of the family money was wasted on wine, women, gambling, or wild living, but had been carefully husbanded and passed from generation to generation. While other families gained reputations for having some bad apples on their family tree, the Farr family was unsullied. It also meant they were quite well off and would be able to survive into the future.

For the first few days, Richard walked around Houston and rode the horse-drawn busses which carried multiple passengers on set routes. He was looking for a boarding house close to where he would be working. A quiet street on the west of Buffalo Bayou had just the place.

His landlady, Abigail Johnson, was a spinster. Her mother and father had left her the house she lived in and very little money to live on, so renting out rooms made sense. The area of town was quiet and most of the people who lodged with her were professionals just starting their careers. Richard fit well with the young lawyer from Boston, a new doctor trained in Edinburgh, and a banker from New York. There was a couple who lived on the top floor, an older lady who had a room down the hall from Richard, and an old man just back from foreign lands as a missionary.

The room he rented was in the back and overlooked a neat garden. The house had a large main parlor, a generous- sized dining room, and a modern bath. The food was good and plentiful too. Meals were at set times and if they were missed, there was no refund and no leftovers. Richard always made sure to tell Miss Johnson when he would not be in for a meal.

On one of his trips to the center of town, he purchased some rough cotton trousers called Levis, a heavy cotton shirt, leather jacket, and leather work gloves. He had seen pictures of cowboys in the dime novels small boys liked to read but thought it would be best to see them in person before deciding to purchase anything. After meeting one in the bar of the Cattleman's Hotel, he felt confident about his purchases. Richard was in Texas on business and did not need to be seen as a joke by anyone.

The next Saturday morning, Richard left early to meet Mr. Chadwick. After two trolley rides and a walk of a few blocks, he arrived at the hotel. The desk clerk told him the man he wanted to meet was in the dining room having his breakfast. When he was asked what Mr. Chadwick looked like, the desk clerk just said, "He is one of a kind, sir."

The room was full and standing just inside the door, Richard surveyed the room, looking for a man who would fit the clerk's description. Almost immediately, he saw to whom the clerk must have been referring. At a small round table in the back of the big room sat a huge man with bright red hair. As Richard walked up to the table, the man put his knife and fork down, chugged some of the beer he had in front of him, wiped his hands on his pants, and stood up to greet him. Richard was well over six feet tall, but John Chadwick made him look average in height. Close-up, he could also see the man's face and what was showing of the rest of his skin was covered in a mass of freckles. However, the most startling thing about him, besides his size, was the red, almost orange hair.

Richard put out his hand and introduced himself. "You must be John Chadwick, and I am Richard Farr. It is good to finally meet you."

John took his hand and shook it hard, but not out of malice; it was all his massive hands knew. "Good to meet you too. Everybody just calls me Red or Big Red. Well, you can tell why. My mother was from Denmark and said she was full-blooded Viking, descended from Eric the Red or somebody. Anyway, Maw died when I was just a kid, so I never really understood it very well. It just explains the really red hair on me and on my sister." He reached around and pulled a chair up to his little table.

"So sit down and we'll talk and have something to eat." Richard complied. A waiter came with a plate of food, a mug of beer, and then left them alone. He hadn't ordered the food, but the big steak, eggs, and portion of bread looked too good to pass up. The beer, however, was another matter. For breakfast? American customs were sometimes hard to understand.

For the next hour, the two men talked and ate. The English group who was investing in the Chadwick cattle ranch simply wanted to see where their money was going and get some kind of accounting of the herd upon which the investment was based.

The waiter had taken the empty plates away and "Red" Chadwick was rolling a smoke in his big hands. "You see, the problem is, them cows are all on the range. We count what we take to market, and I can give you an estimate of how many cows and bulls are out there, but an exact count would be difficult. I understand in England you can count your stock because it is in nice, neat little pastures, but here, well, some ranches are as big as countries. I just think you need to see for yourself."

This was what Richard had expected to hear. The time he had waited for the meeting with Red Chadwick had been spent listening and talking to the men he had met in the Cattlemen's Hotel. Most of the men had been happy to answer his questions—well, at least once they got past his accent and formal clothes. One man, an older cattleman named Jeremy Higgins, had been especially helpful.

Richard and Red agreed they would travel to the Chadwick ranch in two days' time. The ranch was located almost due west and the new Houston to San Antonio train would take them part way. The rest of the trip would be north of Columbus about forty miles up to a little place called Round Top, and would be accomplished on horseback.

Richard paid for an extra two months at Miss Abigail Johnson's boarding house, had a final dinner with Jeremy Higgins, and prepared to venture into the wilds of Texas.

———⟫⟪⟨⟩⟫⟪———

The dinner with Mr. Higgins was very informative. "I understand the need to bring capital in to expand herds and upgrade operations on some of these big spreads, but listen to what you are being told and look very carefully. Raising cows in Texas is just not the same as in England. We have long, lean cows with big horns for a reason, and even though they don't have as much meat on them as your short-legged, compact English cows, they are built to live on the range. Our cows have to forage among tall weeds and stickers, wade seasonal creeks, and those horns are good for fighting off predators. No, our cows may not be as pretty, but they will live through a lot that yours wouldn't." Jeremy had struck on something he was hearing from his English investors: crossing the Texas cows with English bulls to increase meat production. He had seen some bulls offloaded at the port and recognized Herefords, Angus, and Jersey breeds. The man at the port told him the Angus and Herefords were for beef while the Jersey would be going north to dairy herds.

Mr. Higgins continued, "I know these fancy bulls will make us some fine, beefy steers, but it's the birthing and the survival that make the difference. The short, stocky calves are hard on the cows and more are lost in birthing than are the regular longhorn or the longhorn mix. And, when you mix them with the longhorn, well, these lean cows are just not designed to have big calves."

Jeremy continued, "I have been out on the range with my cows during calving season, and they don't need no help. They just drop 'em with no problem, but with these mixes, you have to help 'em or you can lose both the cow and the calf."

Richard understood what the man was saying, but he was going to have to convince the moneymen in London. "You also talked about surviving on the range. Don't all cows fight for their young?"

Mr. Higgins chuckled. "It's not just looking after their young. You just don't want to get in the way of a cow with a large rack of horns when she wants to fight off a wolf or coyote. She'll sweep her head from side to side and she'll gore whatever is in her way. No, a cow will protect her young, but also herself."

Richard had a lot to think about; the information was filed away and would be used to convince the men in London. Aside from some advice on buying a horse, the older man wished him a safe journey.

———⇒»《◉》«⇐———

Before they made the trip, Red had told Richard to bring a horse with him on the train. Red's horse was in the livery behind the hotel and it would travel in the stock car. Richard and Red visited the horse brokers near the train station to find a suitable mount for the trip.

Richard had ridden all his life and thought of himself as a good horseman. He understood about the different kinds of saddle he would be using, but found the buying of a horse perplexing. In England, the saddle was not terribly expensive, but the horse usually was, especially if it was from a good bloodline or trained for hunting. In Texas, the saddle was turning out to be more expensive than the horse. A bay gelding looked all right to Richard, but Red walked right past it and took the halter of a little roan. The horse was a few inches shorter than the one Richard liked, and when he asked Red about it, he got his first lesson in buying a mustang.

Red led the horse over to the fence and tied it to a rail. "Look at the chest. It's broad so he will have strength and stamina. Also, see the way this horse looks bloated." He pointed to the bay. "It's probably had some bad feed, and the chance it will go colicky is real high. No, you want this little horse."

Richard noted everything Red said and admitted he had to agree with the assessment. However, before the deal concluded, Richard insisted on riding the little roan outside of the corral. The saddle creaked as he put it on, but the horse felt good to him and he decided to take him.

The train would be leaving in the morning and Richard wanted to stay one more night at the boarding house. He put his things in order, sent a letter to the investors in London, and got what he knew would be his last good night's sleep in a bed until he would get to the ranch house on the Chadwick Ranch.

———✦———

Richard and Red stood on the wooden landing of the train stop in Columbus, Texas, with their horses as they watched the train disappear into the distance. Music came from a rundown Mexican Cantina across the tracks and the telegraph office was deserted. The only thing in Columbus proper that was lit-up was the saloon.

The two men tied their horses in front of the bar and took their belongings inside with them. One of the men inside recognized Red and made a place for them at his table. A man in a soiled apron asked if they wanted something to eat. While they waited for their food, Red took the horses to the livery in the back and put them up for the night. The men would leave at sunrise.

The area they traveled was not the desert that Richard expected, but it was an area of rolling hills with thick scrub and trees. The ranch where they were going had live water or natural springs or rivers that did not dry up in the summer unless Texas was having a drought. While it was green, it was not the kind of "green" a cow/calf unit would find nutritious.

For two and a half days, they rode until they came to a place called Round Top. Red told Richard it was named for a hill formation and the ranch was on the other side. Richard didn't know how Red knew it; there were no fences, gates, or signs to mark the boundary, but as they crossed over onto the Chadwick Ranch, Red told him they were just about home.

As they crested a small rise, Red pointed to the buildings tucked up close to the hills on the west side of a shallow valley. Richard could make out a modest home, barn, stock pens, and assorted outbuildings. As Red pointed them out, all were positioned to take advantage of the protection afforded by the hills.

"This area of Texas gets a lot of really bad storms, called tornados. Tornados can blow up out of a storm within several minutes and go away just as fast, but it can pull a cow up and twirl it around, then slam in back down. You don't want to be anywhere near a tornado. I got a cellar we get into if we see one, but you don't always know when one is coming, and if you are out on the range, well, best to just get into a ditch or gully and hold on!"

The closer they got to the house, the more Richard could see of it. No extra money was going into high living if the home was any indication. The paint, what there was of it, was peeling and some wood shingles on the roof needed to be patched. As he looked the place over, a girl with flaming red hair came to the porch, shielded her eyes from the sun, and when she saw the big man next to Richard, started waving.

A man came from one of the barns and took their horses while Red made the introductions. "Richard, this is my little sister, Elbeth."

Richard took her proffered hand and looked at the owner. Nature had been kind to this brother and sister. Where Red's skin was a mass of dark red freckles, Elbeth had creamy skin with just a touch of light freckles on her high cheekbones and across the bridge of her nose. While her hair was the same red, she had brushed and combed it into a liquid copper color and secured it into a bun at the base of her neck, but the most striking feature was her eyes. Richard was sure he had never seen such sapphire-blue eyes in his life.

Elbeth bid them come in and have something to eat. The house's interior was very different from the outside. The plank floors looked clean, were highly polished, and there were homemade rugs under the wood furniture. The walls had whitewash to brighten them and windows to let in the light. Everything looked and smelled fresh.

Red took Richard to a room off the main one that had a bed, chair, dresser, and table by the bed. The bed sported a homemade quilt and looked inviting after two nights of sleeping outside. However, before eating, Red led him to the back porch and a sink with a pump where they could both wash off the dust and dirt from the journey from their hands and faces.

The kitchen had a huge wood stove and a long wooden table. Red told his guest all of the cowhands ate their meals together, and Elbeth did the cooking with the help of a Mexican girl who lived on the ranch. Half or more of the men who worked for Red were either Mexican or freed slaves. The food was simple fare but well cooked, and the coffee was strong and hot. Elbeth and the girl, Dominica, served the men, and then Elbeth sat to have coffee and hear about her brother's trip.

Richard was only half listening to the sibling banter until he heard his name. "Mr. Farr, what are they like?"

He realized he hadn't heard the question, but so did Red. "Aw, Elbeth, can't you see the man is tired? Anyways, maybe he don't know anything about women's dresses."

Richard came to her rescue. "I'm not so tired I can't answer the ladies' question. So you want to know what the women in London are wearing? They would follow what the Queen or her court wear, but the Queen is still in mourning for her husband and rarely seen. Her son, Crown Prince Edward, has a very fashionable wife and moves in a trendy circle of friends. They set the fashion."

"The Crown Prince started the fashion of wearing, for dinners or small parties, a black jacket and tie instead of the more formal white tie and tail coat. The women have kind of flowing silk or satin dresses with bustles. There are some popular magazines that have excellent sketches of the ladies and you could see what they look like, but I wouldn't know where to get one out here." Like many men, he wasn't into fashion or the talk of it, so after his short statement on the matter, he went quiet as he looked around.

Red figured it was time to move the discussion outside. Richard thanked Elbeth for the meal and followed his host. They walked past the bunkhouse where the cowhands slept, a small cottage where Dominica and her Mexican family lived, and on to the barn and stock pens. While none of the buildings were painted or whitewashed, they were in decent repair.

Inside the barn was an older man who Red introduced as Juan. He was Dominica's father and took care of the stock in the barns, any leather goods like saddles or bridles, and had taught Red and his sister to ride when they were children.

Red elaborated, "Dad was busy out on the range with the cattle when we was little, and Maw took care of all of us and the little ones. Juan would put us up on a pony or one of the two-year-olds and let us get the feel of a horse. We have spent a lot of years in the saddle, my sister and me, and it all started with his teaching."

Richard picked up on the family remark. "You said little ones. You have younger brothers or sisters?"

Red looked down. "Richard, this is a hard land, a good land, but a hard land. At one time, there were more of us. I was the second boy, but my older brother died of the typhus when he was six and I was about four. We had a sister between me and Elbeth, but she didn't live beyond the birthing. A brother, who died of smallpox, came after Elbeth. It was the same smallpox epidemic, which took Maw and the new baby girl. No, you go to any ranch around here and we all got our cemeteries filled with the cost of settling the land."

Red hadn't spoken of his father, but Richard was curious. "And you father, what about him?"

The man straightened to his full height. "Died of dysentery before he could get home from the war. Andersonville was not the healthiest of places." Red went on, "This part of Texas was mostly German descent, and they didn't hold with owning slaves. When the war started, many Texans joined the fight on the Confederate side, but quite a few fought for the North. Paw was captured and sent to Andersonville as part of his punishment for being a traitor to the Southern cause. Seems they didn't think a Texan should choose on which side to fight."

The sun was just starting to set behind the house when the men finished the tour of the outbuildings. The last places they walked were near the garden Elbeth kept and the fruit tree orchard. Red stopped before a couple of wooden doors in the ground. He opened one side and a set of steps could be seen going down into a dark hole.

"This is the cellar where we keep the fruit, vegetables, and some of the preserved foods Elbeth puts up for the winter. It is also the storm shelter, and if you see a storm coming, don't stop, just get in here. Your life may depend on what you do."

The girl, Dominica, could be seen going to the back porch of the house and ringing the dinner bell. From the barn, the bunkhouse, and the stock pens, four men of various shades of brown and black made for the house. The men all started with a good wash, and Richard and Red joined them.

Red introduced Richard to the men he hadn't seen earlier in the afternoon and mentioned two men who were still out riding the range. They wouldn't be back until the next day at the earliest, and the group all sat down at the kitchen table to eat. "This is the usual number we keep here, but when we need them for roundup or trailing to the rail siding, we might have as many as fifteen men working here." Richard enjoyed the talk around the table. He didn't say much or ask many questions, but he was learning, and one thing he had learned in school—"it's hard to learn when your mouth is open"—he remembered and absorbed what these men had to say.

Plans were made for Red to take Richard for an extended survey of the ranch. A wagon was going with them to carry food, their sleeping rolls, and other items they might need. Two men would also go along with six extra horses. Each man would ride and lead a horse. Two would be tied to the back of the wagon and two horses would pull the wagon. The group would start out early the day after next.

The following day was spent preparing for the trip. They would be sleeping outside on the ground, but the weather was nice and Richard wasn't concerned. He had a bedroll he had purchased at the store in Houston where he bought his cotton shirt and trousers. Red had shown him how to tie everything up to make it easy to attach to the back of the saddle.

Elbeth baked several extra pans of biscuits and the wagon was loaded with food for Juan to cook on the trail. From the cellar, he put some apples, late melons, and some chilies in with the small bags of flour, sugar, beans, sausages, bacon, and coffee. Everything was packed in a barrel strapped to one side of the wagon, and a water barrel was hung from the other side. Tinder, some dry firewood, and horse feed were put in the back of the rig.

The early morning light hadn't crept above the low hills before the men were dressed, washed, and seated at the table for the breakfast Elbeth had cooked. Slabs of beef, eggs, biscuits, grits, potatoes fried in bacon fat with onions, and strong coffee would hold the men until mid-day. Each man also had a soft leather bag of cornbread, cheese, and dried beef hanging from the pommel of his saddle in case of hunger. Two canteens of water and a bag with horse feed for the mount also hung from the saddle.

Each man had a scabbard with a rifle, several bullet rounds, and a box of spares in their bags. Red had tried Richard's marksmanship the first day after they left the train siding at Columbus and was surprised he was such a good shot. "Men and women here learn to shoot almost before they can sit their own horse, but I didn't think you would need to in England. We do it for protection and to eat, but why there?"

Richard thought about this one. True, his family had their own forests where the game was for their pleasure to hunt if they wanted, and many did. Others simply kept the forest creatures for show and allowed their gamekeepers to cull them when necessary. He couldn't remember when the last poacher had been tried for "stealing" the Lord's deer or pheasant, but on some estates it was still done.

He had learned to hunt and shoot from his father's game-keeper when he was a child and had shot some birds as a boy, but when he was invited to other friend's homes, he was often expected to stalk or shoot and was happy he knew how. In Texas, however, he knew these men hunted to fill the pot or in the case of a preda-tor, to protect themselves or their stock. His little experience with shooting was nothing compared to the necessity of the men who rode the range or the women who took birds or a hare to fill a pot to feed a family.

The men discussed the differences as they rode along and Richard found himself, more and more, gaining a profound respect for what it took to live on the frontier. When he finished with a day's riding on his father's estate, there was a stableman to take his horse, walk, clean, curry, and put it in the stalls. If his boots were soiled, they were cleaned and polished before he put them on again, and so were his clothes. If a button went astray or a shirt cuff lost a stitch, someone mended it for him.

He had gotten handy with a thread and needle and could put a button on or clumsily darn a sock or fix a collar. His boots and shoes were his responsibility and he knew where every good shoesh-ine stand was if he wanted someone to do it for him. His new horse, if he took it back to Houston, would stay in the stable behind the boarding house when he returned, and it would be his place to take care of him or have the boy Miss Johnson had living there do it for him, for a price. Taking care of yourself was a lot of trouble and he hadn't even tried cooking yet.

Richard knew he would have to think about getting married one day, but he was not settled yet and could not envision bringing a lady into his life. Like the other men in his family, he did not spend his time in the "soft" pursuits of flirting, dancing, or mild conversation. When he was ready for a wife, he would look for one, but until then, he would work to build his life.

———◎———

Elbeth looked out of the window over her kitchen sink. She was lucky to have a pump in the house. Most homes on the frontier did not have such a luxury, but it was something her daddy had done to make her mom's life easier. The window was actually not cut in until later, to let in light, and it had glass, which had been shipped all the way from Kansas City.

She wasn't much for daydreaming, but she did think a lot while she did chores. With most of the men gone, it was easier for Dominica and her to cook for those left behind, but there was still the garden which needed tending and some sewing to catch up. Right now, however, her thoughts were taken up with Richard.

She had never been treated as he treated her. When she got up to get something from the stove, he stood up; when she sat down, he was up again. He called her Miss Chadwick and never wore his hat inside and especially not at the table. He was a gentleman, and he treated her just like she imagined he would treat a lady.

This had never happened to her and she liked it. Oh sure, he was not a rancher and didn't really understand what the life of a rancher was, but did she want to spend her life as a rancher's wife? Right now, she kept house for her brother, but some day she wanted her own life with a husband and some children.

He was handsome, anybody could see he was, and tall. She liked the way he looked and with the way his clothes fit, well, she figured he was also pretty strong. Of course, putting him up against her brother, Richard was not as big or tall, but her brother was larger than anybody she knew. No, he looked like he would make a fine husband when he got around to getting married. Maybe Red would talk to him about her, maybe so.

———◎———

The tour of the ranch lasted for almost a week. Each morning, Juan would have a hearty breakfast prepared by the time they got up and saw to their horses. Before the sun rose, they would be fed and ready to set off. Juan would then pack his wagon and head for the next campsite to cook dinner and maybe put a pie on to bake to accompany the meal. The men would take biscuits, meat, and cheese with them to eat during the day from horseback, but by the time dinner rolled around, they would be able to smell the good food Juan had ready.

Richard was impressed with the size of the ranch, the stock, and the fact it had water. He also saw some animals he had never heard of and one, the rattlesnake, he could go without seeing for the rest of his life. For the most part, however, he was pleased with what he saw. His report to the investors in London would show his enthusiasm for the venture, but also explain to them the problems of ranching on the frontier of Texas.

By the time the group returned to the ranch house, Richard was saddle tired and ready to rest for a couple of days. Red and the other men needed to get back to work. Richard had planned to be on the ranch with Red for at least a month, but days stretched to weeks and then to more than the month. The work on the ranch was hard, but Richard enjoyed pitching in and working alongside the other men. It puzzled Red at first; this man was a gentleman, and gentlemen were not usually known for doing hard physical labor. He then looked at how Richard interacted with Elbeth, but decided this had not changed from the day of Richard's arrival. No, it seemed to Red the man just enjoyed the work and the life on the ranch.

A week before his rent at the boarding house was due, Richard sat down to breakfast and told Red it was time he got back to Houston. The men made plans for Juan to take Richard in the wagon to the rail siding in Columbus, but the horse, which was bought for the trip, would stay on the ranch. "Red, if you'll have me back, I'd like to come when you have roundup, and this little horse might be just the thing for me to ride."

Red was happy to hear this and wanted him to return. "Elbeth and I liked having you here and will look forward to it. Just let me know and somebody will be in Columbus to get you."

———

Richard arrived at the boarding house and found a pile of mail on the small desk in his room. He had written to the moneymen in London and told them he would be going to the ranch to have a look at the operation. He had expected to see mail from them, but he was surprised to find several pieces from his family.

He put the business ones aside and opened the mail from his family. The oldest letter was from his mother. In neat, flowing script, she informed Richard his father had suffered from a fall during a hunt at a nearby estate and had died instantly. He read past the initial shock where she described the funeral and people who had attended. The bishop had officiated and his brother, the newly ordained priest at the home church, had assisted.

Richard set the letter to the side. True, he had left his home to come to America, probably to stay and establish himself, but he thought, deep down, he always expected his family to be at "home" in England. They were never supposed to change and he knew, if things did not work out, he could always return. Now, his father was dead, his mother a widow, and his oldest brother, Harold, was the new Viscount of Gibbons. He had been close to his father and his brothers. Unlike some families, the boys had grown up in the family home. It was more cost-effective to have a tutor live in the house and teach them than send them all to boarding school. It was easy to hire a newly hooded don from Oxford to spend a couple of years in the schoolroom his mother had set aside next to the nursery.

Every couple of years, a new graduate was hired to replace the old one and as the boys grew, the lessons got harder and harder. At sixteen, his second brother, Roland, left for Sandhurst to take up his military training and then the commission his father had bought him. It was at this point the two remaining boys, Edgar and Richard, were sent to St. Allard's, to prepare for Oxford.

The second letter was from his brother, Harold, and bore the family crest. The paper and seals may have been formal, but the letter was warm and filled with concern for his youngest sibling. Harold had been with his father on the hunt and was able to give Richard more details as to what happened.

Richard's father and brother had been at Aldwin, the home of the Oswin family. They were the closest neighbors to the Farr's and had a long history together. Two brothers who were Norman Knights had seized both the Farr and Oswin family estates during the "Conquest." Neither one of the brothers had any children, but through various vehicles used by the local clergy, the original Anglo-Saxon families, the Oswins and Farrs, were able to retain their names and estates. Harold described the rains that had softened the grounds over which the hunt had been ridden. Their father had just purchased a fine Irish hunter from a local gypsy horse trader and wanted to try him. The father had been warned about the risk over an unstable surface with a new mount, but he was adamant. All went well until nearly the end, when the fox they had been chasing circled back and the hounds turned. While the other riders were able to turn their mounts with little trouble, the big hunter had the bit in his teeth and shied from the field. A seven-foot hedge was the only thing to stop him, but the force of the sudden stop flung the Viscount of Gibbons over his head and his neck broke on impact.

Harold had wanted to destroy the horse where he stood, but was urged to sell him to another member of the hunt before his father's body could be removed from the field. Three stable hands from Aldwin brought a board, put his father's body on it, and carried him back to the manor house. Harold had a wagon take their father on to Farr Cottage, and the funeral was held in the home church.

As Richard put his brother's letter aside, he could feel the sadness his brother conveyed. He knew Harold would be moving his wife into the position his mother had enjoyed, the children would be put in line to inherit, and he and his two older brothers moved beyond the main family group. Richard's mother would either remain in the Cottage or move to a small house or "Dower House," where she would have her own household, albeit smaller, than she had been used to in the Cottage.

The next letter was from his second brother, Roland, and was a simple note with his feelings on his father's death and well wishes for his absent brother. He did have the news he would be leaving to join his regiment in India before monsoon season. Roland promised to write as soon as he was in his new post.

The last of the family letters was from the Reverend Edgar Charles Farr, St. Alban's Church. The cleric in the family was more concerned with their father's eternal soul, how their mother's grieving process was moving along, and in recounting his memories of their father. He also had the news a Miss Marjorie Llewellyn of Hillscombe House, third daughter to Lord and Lady Edward Llewellyn, had agreed to be his wife. The wedding, of course, would have to wait for at least a year after his father's death. Both families were happy.

Richard had not been away from his boarding house room for even two months, but so many things in his life had changed. Before he looked at the business letters, he wanted to get something to drink, relax, and think about the alterations his English family had endured. Normally, Miss Abigail Johnson didn't like her boarders having anything to drink, besides water, in their rooms. He, however, had a hipflask with some good brandy in it for shock and decided this was shock enough to qualify.

He unscrewed the large cap which also served as a shot cup and poured himself a draught. This was the last of the brandy he had gotten from the family reserves before he left home, and it seemed fitting for him to drink it in a salute to his father while he pondered the changing tide of family fortunes. In his mind's eye, he also reflected on the life he had had with his father and the realization he would never see or hear him again pushed home. He downed part of the brandy and cried for his loss.

Sometime later, he looked at the desk and the pile of business letters. There was no time like the present to look at them, and he reached for the biggest one. As he had already suspected, it was from the moneymen in London and had missives from each of the partners. He read each of them as well as a couple questionnaires written by their lawyers and knew the information he had brought back from his visit to the ranch would answer all they wanted or needed to know. There were also a couple of other business letters in the pile, but they did not seem important.

The last letter was at the bottom of the stack, and had a lawyer's name he did not recognize. The address was in London and located somewhere in the financial area known as the City. It contained just two separate letters, the second of which was more than one page.

The first was a cover letter that explained who the attorney was and that his father had retained him at the time Richard left for America. "I regret hearing the news about the Viscount's passing, but your father left some business that needed to be addressed upon his death." The balance of the letter described how his father had left Richard a small inheritance, apart from his overall estate, which would pass to the next Viscount in line. This was the subject of the second part of the letter.

Richard pulled the second part out of the envelope and looked it over. It was written in his father's own hand and in it he expressed his wishes that his son would find adventures in America to be exciting and fruitful. He told him how proud he was of him and he wished there was some way Richard could share in the inheritance, but since everyone knew this was impossible, he was setting some money aside, outside of the estate, for him to use to build his future.

"My son, you have a fine mind and good sense. The business you have with the men in London is satisfactory, but at some time in the future, you may wish to go forth on your own. I may not be alive to help you when the time comes so please find the sum of 5,000 pounds sterling* credited to your account upon my passing."

In addition, it was signed, "your loving father, Sir Arthur Roland Farr, 15th Viscount of Gibbons."

The flask was emptied as Richard finished reading his father's note. He had never expected to receive anything from his father or family upon the death of his father. Even if there was to be an inheritance, he could not have imagined the huge sum, about which his father had written. He had anticipated, like other non-inheriting sons, the most he might receive other than a notice his father had passed away was perhaps some small token. In one fell swoop, his father had secured him a life of independence. He would need to think carefully about what he would do.

*25,000 in American dollars of the day, a princely sum!

The trip back to Houston from the Chadwick Ranch had been long and tiring. The added stress of the news he received along with the brandy made sleep easy for him. The next day was a Sunday and he would be in time to attend services at the little church down the street. Richard, like all of his family, was Anglican and a regular churchgoer. The church he was currently attending was Methodist and was not the same with, although similar to, Anglican doctrine. He hoped to find a suitable church in the future, but right then, sleep was catching up to him.

This Sunday, he visited Jeremy Higgins. The older cattleman had a small ranch, which could be reached by the same rail line Richard had used to come from Columbus. Jeremy's sons ran the main ranch, a huge operation south of San Antonio, and it was to the smaller ranch the sons would move their cattle when they wanted to reach the railhead.

The ranch house was a big Victorian Jeremy had built for his wife. After years of living in dry, barren areas, he wanted her to have all the luxury he could afford, and Jeremy could afford a lot. Richard had rented a horse at the station to make the trip to the little ranch. He had never been to visit at the "Lazy H" before, but he had been invited many times. The trip up the long dusty road to the lush green lawns was surprising. He was more amazed when his host told him his "little" ranch was just a little more than twenty thousand acres.

Jeremy sent one of his stablemen back to the station with Richard's rented horse and insisted his guest at least stay the night. The two men settled down for a long conversation in the main salon. Richard told Jeremy about his father's passing, the long trip to the Chadwick ranch, and finally the inheritance. His host listened quietly, asking a few questions here and there, before he gave his opinion. Richard probed him about what he thought would be the best investment, and Jeremy asked for further information.

"Richard," Jeremy began, "you are a young man, and while the amount your father left you is a sizeable sum, it will not be enough to set you up for life. You will need to work and from what I have seen of you, it should be something you would want to do. However, I don't think ranching is what you would be good at. You have your contacts in London, and even though they have men there who like to invest in their former colonies, you may also wish to make yourself known in New York."

"The foreign contacts you have, the fact you're conversant with aspects of ranching, and the obvious familiarity you have with numbers, well, in my book you would make a very good banker. In fact, if you were to partner with an already established bank or open your own, I would like to be one of your first customers."

The older man's enthusiasm, confidence, and suggestion took Richard by surprise. True, he had worked in an investment office of a bank in London when he first came down from Oxford, but he hadn't thought about making it a career. The moneymen who had brought him in had found him through the bank and had given him the opportunity to grow beyond the bank. Now, the prospect of doing the same work, but in a different place on earth with a different set of skills, wasn't totally unpleasant.

Something Richard had learned about himself when he was on the Chadwick Ranch was he was more than a paper and desk man, but he also knew he would never be a rancher or do the kind of day-to-day work a rancher would need to do to be successful. No, he was no "gentleman" rancher, but neither was he a "green-eyeshade" clerk.

Jeremy Higgins watched the thought process of his young visitor. He had seen several eastern or foreign "dudes" come through

Texas thinking they knew everything, but not this man. He was intelligent enough to know when he didn't know something and when to ask questions. Richard was smart, but he was also smart enough to learn. Jeremy knew of many people who had come west to seek their fortunes only to find the differences between "farming" in the east or Europe was very different from "ranching" in Texas or the territories. Most failed, but the man sitting in front of him was made of sterner stuff and cut from a different cloth. Richard could succeed.

Nothing was decided that evening, but the next few days gave Jeremy the opportunity to have long talks with the young man. It also allowed him the occasion to introduce Richard to a niece of his wife's who was also staying at the ranch.

Jeremy had married up, way up, when he found his Abbey. She had been the oldest daughter of an Englishman who had settled a big ranch up north along the Red River. She was petite and looked so delicate, but she was all determination. Her father was one of those younger sons like Richard and he had come to America to find his fortune. This he did, and his would have been one of the biggest ranches in Texas if ill health and no living sons had not forced him to divide it.

Abbey, or Abigale if you wanted to be formal, had been the oldest of four girls. Her mother and father had two sons and another daughter, but those three children had died within days of their birth. Her mother did not live more than two weeks after the last boy was born. George Montgomery, her father, could not continue after he took sick with a heart condition, and he deeded his ranch to the husbands of his married daughters. Jeremy had a goodly portion of the ranch, and one of his sons was currently running it.

Lucinda Louise Langley was the second daughter of Abbey's sister Dora. She had grown up on the ranch, but had also attended Mrs. Ashley's Boarding School for Young Ladies in Boston. She could ride, rope, and cook over an open fire, but she could also play the pianoforte, sing, paint, and do fancy embroidery. Her skills of pouring tea, engaging in light dinner conversations, and running a household were evident in Jeremy's own house.

His Abbey was doing poorly, health-wise, and Miss Lucinda— or Lucy, as they called her— did the work of the chatelaine of the house. On most ranches, the men ran the outside, but it was the women who lorded over the inside, and Miss Lucy did it very well.

Lucy also had the good looks of the Montgomery girls. Abbey and her sisters were well known for their fine figures, porcelain daintiness, and beautiful countenances. Growing up the way they did, they also had kind hearts and proper manners. Yes, Jeremy had definitely married up when he married his Abbey, and Miss Lucy was a credit to his wife's family.

He had introduced Richard to Miss Lucy when he first sat down to talk to the young man and had hoped there might be a spark there, but so far, nothing. He knew the boy was okay with women, he had seen the girls at the bar in the Cattlemen's Hotel talking to him, and he seemed to like them. However, like many men, he knew to be wary of entanglements with any of the bargirls, even for one time; it could ruin the rest of a man's life. Maybe the boy just wasn't ready to be looking for a wife yet.

By Tuesday, the men shook hands at the station and Richard boarded the train back to Houston. Jeremy had given him the names of a couple of men who might be looking to take in partners in their banks. He had also advised him to make the trip to New York soon to begin making connections there.

Richard had enjoyed his few days with Jeremy and had a lot about which to think. The idea of going back into the banking business was double-edged. He had worked in a banking house in London and found it not to his liking. However, it did give him the necessary training to do the work of a banker. The other aspect was the idea it would be "his" bank, or if he was partnered—which he preferred—he would have a substantial stake, and at least it would be his to make into a successful venture.

Within a few days of returning to Houston, he had sent his report to the men in London about his trip to the Chadwick Ranch and made appointments to see the men Jeremy had advised him to visit. The first man gave Richard a strange feeling, almost as if he wanted to wash after shaking his hand. The man was interested in the idea of a partner, but not a "working" partner, just a give-me-your-money-and-I-will-do-the-rest type of partner. This was not what Richard wanted, and he thanked the man for his time and left.

The second gentleman was older than Jeremy and was the sole owner of his own banking house. He had been in Houston for several years and served a small community of people who were all Jewish. Many of the other banks would not deal with them, and Samuel Newhouse, a native of New York, had opened the bank to cater to their needs. He had one unmarried granddaughter and no other relatives living in Houston. He was interested in what Richard had to say.

The two men met in the small office that housed the "bank" Mr. Newhouse ran. It was small and located on the second floor of an office building in the commercial part of downtown. The bank only catered to the Jewish community, and they knew where to find him, so there was no need to have a street-side office or do any advertising. One of the first things Samuel Newhouse needed to know from Richard was if he would have a problem with the current patrons.

Richard had never been in close, daily contact with Jews before, but it didn't mean he had never done business with them. Some very wealthy men in London were Jews who made their living from loaning money to the gentry who cared more for keeping up appearances than being fiscally responsible. More than one titled scion of an ancient family had sat before him asking for money to pay back the Jewish moneylenders, usually with very little luck or success.

For Richard, he did not see a problem with the current clientele. He had no prejudice either for or against Jews as a people. The men Samuel Newhouse served were mostly from either New York or Boston families or a few German Jews who had emigrated just after the American Civil War. They had thriving businesses, worked hard, had solid families, and from what Samuel said, were devout to their religion. Why would he object to people who were so stable?

⟶⟫⟨⟩⟪⟵

During the next few weeks, Richard met several times with Samuel Newhouse and at times, some of his clients. Richard knew he was on probation and understood the reasons for it. For such a closed community, it was difficult to allow an outsider to enter. He decided the best course of action was just to be himself.

Jeremy also visited Houston during this time and sat in on more than one of the meetings. Richard watched the interaction between Samuel and Jeremy and could see they were not just business acquaintances, but friends. After one particularly long meeting, Richard asked him about it. Jeremy invited Richard to lunch the next day to explain things to him about his friendships.

Jeremy had taken a private dining room at the Cattleman's so he and Richard could have a long, private conversation. The waiter brought each course quietly into the room, knowing the men having lunch did not want to be disturbed by too much noise.

"Richard," Jeremy began, "when you came out to the ranch to tell me about your situation, I wanted to make sure you were serious about what you wanted. If you remember, I gave you the names of two bankers who would look favorably on your offer of becoming their partner. Now the first man you went to see is someone I hoped, rightly, with whom you wouldn't enter into a business relationship."

Jeremy took a sip of his drink and went on, "I've done business with him in the past, but although he is not exactly a crooked dealer, well, I always had the feeling he just wasn't very honest. I did business with him once and got out of it as quickly as possible. Now with Samuel, I have known him almost since he first arrived here and count him as a friend."

"I met Samuel when he first arrived in Houston with his family. I used to own some land near the center of town and it had a couple of houses on it. Samuel and his cousin Hiram bought them from me, and it is where they originally had the bank. Hiram left Houston after almost a year because of ill health and later died in California. Samuel and his wife and children stayed, but his wife died of fever. The son married a girl from New York, but they both died of the same fever which took his wife. Samuel has raised his granddaughter, Ruth, since she was six."

Jeremy put more brandy in his glass and continued, "Samuel wants to take Ruth back to New York and find her a suitable husband, but he needs to settle matters at the bank first. I think if the two of you can work out an agreement, this would be your best opportunity. Now, I am not saying Samuel is a pushover, he's not. If you make a deal with him, he will stick to it, but if you leave a loophole, well, he will drive a herd of cattle through it."

Richard had listened to his friend intently. He knew much of what he was being told, having been informed of the particulars by Samuel, but the depth of their friendship was evident in the way Jeremy talked about Samuel. "So, you think it would be the best fit for me? Would he have any problems with my continued work for the men in London or my need to go out to the ranch periodically?"

"Richard, those are things you will have to sort out between you, but just know he is the kind of man who takes his word of honor very seriously, and I think this is what you want in a partner." Jeremy gave the waiter some silver pieces to pay for the dinner and continued when he had left the room. "I believe he will be ready for a firm offer in the next few days. I just want you to be ready to make the decision when the time comes."

The two men left the small private room and made their way to the front door. Richard shook his friend's hand and bid him a good night. As he walked to the livery to get his horse, he thought about the information and advice he had been given.

The next couple of days Richard worked on things for the men in London and responded to correspondence from home. On the third day, he had lunch with Jeremy at a restaurant near the train station. His friend had said he would be going back to the Lazy H on the next day's train and wanted to talk before leaving.

Halfway through the meal, Jeremy had asked all the questions he could think of about the proposed bank business, Richard's other pursuits, and other items of interest, but Richard felt there was something more. Finally, acting slightly nervous, Jeremy got to the missing topic.

"You know, Miss Lucy was asking about you before I came to town. I think the girl likes you. In fact, my Abbey and I were wondering when you would be getting out to visit with us."

Richard looked down at his plate. He had thought about Miss Lucy, but he was not yet settled himself and was not ready to even think about a wife. When he looked back at his friend, he could see the slight apprehension in the man's eyes. "I think Miss Lucy is a fine young lady, but right now, I am not in a position to consider any young woman. If I was, she would be foremost in my mind."

Jeremy was visibly relieved. Since Richard's visit, he had heard nothing from his wife or niece except what a fine husband the young man would make. His Abbey had urged him to feel Richard out to find if he would be interested in Lucy as a wife. At least he had not turned Jeremy down.

"I live in a boarding house, stable my horse in a rented stall, and work off a small table in my room. Before even considering a marriage, I want to be in a position to offer more than a rented life. Please understand, this will not be a long wait, but it will take a few years for me to be in a position to ask a girl for her hand. When the time comes, if Miss Lucy is still available and we have developed an affection for each other, I would be proud to ask you for her hand."

This time, Richard beat Jeremy in paying the bill. Not to be outdone, Jeremy thought for a few minutes, got to his feet, and asked Richard to wait for him. In a short time, Jeremy was back. "Come with me," was all he said.

Out on the street, he saw a wagon tied to a post and Jeremy asked him to get in. "I sent a message along to the ranch that I would be a day late in Houston. There is something I want you to see."

For the next few miles the city gave way to residential streets, on into broad avenues lined with live oaks, and finally to the edge of the town. A couple miles beyond the last big street and house, Jeremy pulled the rig up in a field. On one edge, the waterway known as Buffalo Bayou twisted its way down to the bay and the land had the slight roll of pasture, which was normal for this part of Texas. The area where he had stopped the wagon was on a rise and the rest of the land looked to be dry. Since Houston was built mostly on swampland, it made for a good piece of property. Jeremy just sat for a few minutes, taking in the view.

Richard waited for his friend to tell him why they were sitting in an empty field.

"A couple of years ago, a friend of mine bought this piece of land for his daughter and her fiancé. They were going to be married soon, and he wanted to build them a house here. Only problem was, the man ran off with a woman from New Orleans two months before the wedding. It crushed the girl and he has been trying to sell this for quite some time. It is a good piece of land and works out to just over thirty-seven acres. Now, as you know, it's not big enough to do anything with except build a house and stables on, but it should be worth something someday."

Jeremy continued, "I know he doesn't want much for it, but if I put you in contact with him, the two of you could work it out. It would make a good investment and give you something for building a future.

Richard was looking closely at the land. He had always wanted to have his own property, but it was always far into the future. He didn't know if perhaps it still would be, but he also trusted Jeremy not to give him bad advice. "I like it, but it would be years before I could build a house here. It doesn't have a road to it, much less a street address. I'll talk to the man, but I hope he doesn't want a lot for it."

"I think the two of you can come to an agreement. He had an architect in New York draw up some plans for the site, and he might just throw those in as well. It seems the daughter won't be coming back to live here after all. Her mother found her a guy, with a fancy name, over in Italy and they got married last year." Jeremy took up the reins and the two men headed back to town.

The next day Richard saw his friend off on the train and sought out the man with the land. George Burke was a cattle buyer and had an office near the Cattleman's Hotel. They met in the dining room for lunch and before the meal was over Richard was the proud owner of thirty-seven acres of land on the edge of Buffalo Bayou in a new area called River Oaks. The land had been a sore spot for George, and he was glad to have it off his hands. The plans for the house he was going to build his little girl were tossed in as a gift to Jeremy's friend. For just over $1.25 per acre, Richard had a place to call his own.

With Jeremy back on his ranch, Richard needed to concentrate on his work. He had made an agreement with the men in London and Red Chadwick that he would travel to the ranch twice a year. It had been less than six months since his last trip, but he got a note from Red asking if he wanted to join a roundup and see what it was like.

He wrote letters to London telling them of his plans, and spent a few hours with Samuel before leaving. Samuel agreed to wait on the offer for the bank partnership until he returned. Richard sent a message to Jeremy letting him know where he was and again paid his lodgings in advance. Richard loaded his pack, bedroll, and horse on the train and headed back to Columbus. Dominica's brother, Julio, was at the station when he arrived, and the two men left for the ranch near Round Top the next morning. The miles traveled seemed to clear his head and allowed Richard to think about his future.

He knew he liked Texas and this is where he would stay, but he had determined long ago he didn't think ranching was something he could do on a sustainable basis. Jeremy's wisdom was much appreciated and the advice he had been given about the idea of a bank was how he wanted to proceed, but with one twist—he didn't want to spend all of his time in a dark room counting money. He liked the outdoors and knew he needed the open sky, clear horizons, and feel of a horse beneath him.

Red Chadwick would make him a good ranching customer and Jeremy was already on board, but he would like to find others whom he could get as clients and become friends with in the future. Richard figured he could stand to be indoors most of the time if he had the visits to various ranches to look forward to every so often. The land he had just bought would also help. He wanted to build before the street got to his door or the trolley could clang its bell and break the beautiful silence.

By the time he had reached the ranch, Richard had his next few years planned and was looking forward to getting started. Red and his sister, Elbeth, greeted him like family, and work on the roundup began.

Long days of preparing the chuck wagon and getting the horses ready for the remuda culminated in the beginning of the effort to get all the calves in and ready to take to market. The chuck wagon left the day before the rest of the men, so it would be ready with food and hot coffee for the tired and hungry cowboys. Next, the remuda, controlled by the wrangler, moved with the men so they would have fresh mounts when needed.

A camp was waiting for the men when the first day was over. They would overnight in the first location for at least two days. Each morning, men went out in groups to each of four directions and looked for the calves. For Red, this wasn't just about getting the young steers to market; it was also a chance to count his stock, take a look at the cows and their health, and flag any problems which needed addressing.

The first two days, the men were close enough to the ranch house and the going was easy. It was mostly ground they covered every few weeks when going from one area of pasture to another. By the third day, however, the area wasn't quite as well traveled, and Red warned them to keep a sharp eye out for any problems.

The first potential difficulty came when they found the bones of a cow and calf. Joe Evans, a man known for his tracking and wilderness skills, looked at the area around the remains and decided it was a pack of wolves. On the range, there were predators the ranchers would go out of their way to kill—wolves, mountain lions, and rattlesnakes topped the list. Two men, one of them Joe Evans, left the group and headed out to see if they could find the pack of wolves responsible for the deaths. If they would kill a grown cow and calf, they would not hesitate to kill again.

Rattlesnakes were a constant problem on the range. The smallest baby rattler was lethal and even when dead, an animal with an open sore on their paw or hoof could step on the head, and the poison would kill them. A dead rattlesnake's head was always cut off and buried to keep such a problem from happening. Many people thought the rattlesnake can be heard when it vibrates its tale and the "rattlers" warn of an impending strike. This is not always the case. Sitting down without first looking, finding a spot of shade to rest a horse, or not paying attention to the area around them can lead an unsuspecting victim into trouble.

Richard knew to keep an eye out, he understood to be aware of his surroundings, but things can still happen. Near the end of the roundup, the men and livestock were almost at the greatest distance from the ranch. The chuck wagon was packed up and ready to move to the next campsite for the night when a snake slithered out from a group of rocks and frightened the horse Richard had just mounted. He hadn't quite gotten settled into the seat of his saddle when it happened and he was thrown.

The tail of the snake could just be seen disappearing into a depression under a boulder when the first man reached Richard lying prone on the ground. He wasn't moving but was still breathing. Richard had hit his head on some rocks and his big body hit the ground hard. Nothing seemed to be broken but he lay there, unconscious. Red called for the medical kit Juan carried in the wagon and put some smelling salts under his nose, but he did not come around. Red checked Richard and found no broken bones, only a bad cut on his arm from a bramble bush, but he did breathe funny and was still unresponsive. Red told Juan to make a place in the chuck wagon where he could be laid down, and then he ordered another man to ride to the ranch house and get a wagon to take him back to the ranch. Elbeth would take care of him until they could get the stock on to the railhead and he could get back to the ranch.

Richard's horse was unsaddled and put with the rest of the horses in the remuda, his saddle and bedroll put on the chuck wagon, and Juan moved out to the next campsite. Juan's young son, Jose', sat in the back with Richard and kept a wet cloth on the unconscious man's forehead.

The wagon bounced over the rough ground. Juan tried to make the trip as easy as possible, but it was a chuck wagon, not a fancy carriage or even a stagecoach. The rider Red sent ahead would not be at the ranch until sometime the next day if he rode nonstop, but if he had to quit from exhaustion, it would be the day after that.

Sometime around midday, Juan stopped and checked his passenger. Richard was still out, but his breathing was a little better, and the grimace of pain was not as pronounced as it was before. Juan gave Jose' a fresh canteen of water, and the boy continued putting water on the cloth on Richard's forehead in an attempt to keep him cool.

Richard came around shortly after the chuck wagon stopped. He had a huge bump on his head and substantial bruising on his body, but although nothing was broken, his whole body hurt. Juan gave him a cup of broth and Richard slept shortly after. Jose' continued to sit with him and by the time the cowboys got to the campsite, Richard was again sitting up. His color was almost back to normal.

Red came to sit with him and despite Richard's insistence he would be fine to ride the next day or at least by the day after, his host was adamant he wait for the wagon and go back to the ranch. "You took a very nasty fall and were out for quite some time. Your color is still off and them eyes don't look too clear. Best you go on back to the ranch and Elbeth can look after you for a few days. Some of her cooking and bed rest might be just the thing."

Red would not be persuaded, and Richard gave up trying. He became convinced of the wisdom of what Red was saying when he tried to get up to relieve himself and fell over. If you can't walk, might be you shouldn't ride.

The rider Red sent to the ranch made good time and by the next evening he was at the campsite. True, it was more than twenty-five miles closer than the one he left, but jostling an empty buckboard over scrub and marginal trails was hard on the man and the conveyance. At least the seat had something close to springs to absorb the shock, and it was there Red ordered Richard to ride on the way back.

"Look, we will have the herd to the railhead at Fort Worth in a week or so, the boys will have some fun in town while I sell the stock, and you can recuperate at the ranch while I'm gone. Dominica and her family are there to help Elbeth so she can help you get better. I expect to be back to the ranch in about three weeks."

Red tied Richard's horse to the back of the wagon, Juan gave them a wooden box with some food to eat on the way back, and Juan's son, Jose', was sent with them in case Richard needed some help. The men and the herd moved in one direction and Richard in another.

The trip back to the ranch house gave Richard a chance to think. He needed to get a letter off to Samuel and one to the men in London. The offer with Samuel needed to be finalized as soon as he got back. The man had given him plenty of time to decide, and he needed to let Samuel get to New York and arrange the marriage of his granddaughter.

The men in London were another matter. Seeing the ranch in full operation during a roundup gave him a new perspective about what ranching was and the dangers faced by such an operation. Where the moneymen in London were used to having something they could put their hands on to count, ranching was about what was in the far pasture, on the open range, or estimates of how many calves were ready for market. Most ranches were bigger than the size of London, but with a population of less than a hundred people. It was just difficult to explain or for the men in England to understand.

The roundup had been very successful, and Red was taking more calves to market this year than at any time in the past. He had also told Richard he found his estimate of cows was a little lower than what he had seen on the range. He was worried, however, by the number of wolf attacks and would have to put a bounty on them.

Ranchers often resorted to bounties on predator animals. During the slack times, cowboys would spend time hunting the predators. Presenting either a pelt, tail, or ears, would be enough to collect the bounty. Several times the money earned by collecting bounties was what helped put food on an otherwise sparse table.

The Chadwick ranch was in good financial condition, but would the men in London understand this, or would they be so insistent on bottom-line figures they would miss the true value of the enterprise? Richard would need to work on a very well crafted report to help them see what he had seen.

Elbeth was waiting at the ranch house door when they pulled into the yard. She had put a pot of soup on that morning, aired the bed in the guest room, and was ready to nurse Richard back to health. The look of disappointment on her face at seeing Richard sitting up in the wagon only lasted for a few seconds. Her vision of caring for this handsome man while he fell in love with her was fast retreating. At least her brother was going to be gone for another couple of weeks and Richard could take a turn for the worse; it was known to happen with head injuries.

Richard immediately objected to the idea of going to bed. He was not going to spend his time in a bedroom being an invalid. He was still not very steady on his feet, but he could get from one room to the next without tipping over. Jose' stayed with him and helped him back and forth to the facilities in the backyard. Most of the time, he sat at the table in the kitchen or at Red's desk and worked on the report he would send to London. Before he started that, however, he sent a letter off to Samuel and one to Jeremy.

It was the habit of the ranch to send a wagon to the small village of Round Top at least once a week to get supplies or take the mail and from there, the mail moved by coach to the nearest railroad station. Richard had expected to get a note from Samuel and possibly from Jeremy by the next week or so.

However, Jeremy and another man Richard didn't recognize arrived within days of Jeremy receiving his letter. Richard had been sitting on the porch in the shade and, seeing the two men ride up, had brought Elbeth to the door to see who was coming.

Jeremy had met Elbeth when she was just a little girl, although he did know Red quite well. She recognized the older rancher but was more interested in the man who was with him. Jeremy stepped down from his horse and bid his companion to do the same.

"Richard, well at least you look better than your letter sounded. This here is a young doctor friend of mine, Doc Harris, and he came to make sure that head of yours is all right. Now, why don't you just go inside with the man and let him look you over while I trouble Miss Elbeth for a glass of cool water?"

Elbeth went in with the men and called to Dominica to put more plates on the table for dinner. She sent Richard and the doctor into the bedroom so the exam could be done in private and then got Jeremy a glass of cool water from the well house.

The doctor took his time examining Richard and determined he probably had suffered from a cracked rib, which was healing, and the head wound was doing fine. He was concerned about the time he was unconscious but told Richard that many times a person will come out of a coma but be so deeply asleep that people who are not medically trained will think they are still out.

"The body knows how to heal itself much better than we do. It is possible the coma lasted for less time than was thought, but your body needed time for the wound to heal or begin to heal, and you were just in a deep sleep. Are you having any problems with your vision, or do you notice any differences from before the fall?"

Richard had to think about that one. He had been worried his eyes were starting to go bad before he left to come to the ranch, but after the fall, he was sure of it. He told the doctor and the man looked closer at his eyes.

"Jeremy tells me you are a banker, and this could be the cause of the eyestrain you are having. Still, you should see someone about it when you get to a city big enough for an eye doctor. Houston has a man, but you might want to see someone in a larger city. Any travel plans in the near future?" Richard paused, Jeremy and Samuel had talked to him about going to New York soon, and this would be another reason to make the trip. "I may be going to New York before the end of the year. I guess they might have some good eye doctors there."

"They have some excellent men there. I will give you a couple of names and write a letter of introduction for you. Just let me know when you will be leaving."

Richard put his shirt back on and the doctor closed his bag. Jeremy was sitting on the porch with his cool drink and Elbeth. The doctor gave Jeremy the results of his exam and then it was Richard's turn to ask why they had come.

Jeremy jumped in. "When I got the letter from you, I was worried you had done more damage to that head of yours than anybody knew. Head wounds are bad, I saw too many during the war not to take them seriously. Anyway, it gave me a reason to come out to Red's place. Doc Harris was visiting over at Yancy's ranch and agreed to make the trip with me."

Elbeth left to see to supper, but before she did, she told Jeremy Red should be back in a couple of days. "You' all are welcome to stay until he gets back from Fort Worth. I will send a rider to tell him you're here."

The men all stood when she left the porch. Jeremy thanked her for the invitation and said he and the doctor would be happy to wait for Red's return.

When Elbeth turned to go into the house, she smiled to herself. The doctor Jeremy brought with him, Doc Harris, was a fine-looking man and since nothing would ever probably happen with Richard, she would turn her attention to this new possibility. Besides, he also had red hair!

Red arrived earlier than he had planned on when he sent Richard to the ranch in the wagon to recuperate. The rider Elbeth sent to fetch him found him just a day out and the chuck wagon with Juan only a day behind Red.

Richard had been on Red's mind since the accident. Since the stock sold for a good price, even before he got to Fort Worth, it made for a fast turnaround. A cattle buyer met Red and the herd about a day's ride from Fort Worth and was anxious to purchase the whole lot. The purchaser told him the cattle were needed in Chicago and he offered top-dollar. The men who were with Red all thought it was a fair price, and he was able to pay them off as soon as he got into town. Everybody was happy.

Red had planned on staying a couple of days in Fort Worth to get the herd sold, do some celebrating with the men, and then head home. The business end of the trip was taken care of in record time, and he got a good night's sleep before starting back to the ranch.

Jeremy and Red spent a couple of hours talking about the cattle business and left Elbeth with the two young men. Richard had known of her attraction to him, but with Doc Harris on the scene, he was relieved she had turned her attentions to the doctor. From the looks of it, Harris was already smitten with Elbeth. While the doctor's full head of strawberry-red hair was impressive, the flame-red tresses of Elbeth dwarfed it. Richard figured they would have some very distinctive children.

Richard was getting tired of all the fussing over his health and wanted to get back to Houston. Red and Elbeth saw the three men off from the front porch and the men made their way back to the railhead at Columbus.

Two days after they arrived in Houston, Jeremy witnessed the documents making Richard Farr and Samuel Newhouse partners in a new bank, Newhouse & Farr Bank. Toasts were drunk in the lawyer's office, and Jeremy offered to buy the men dinner to celebrate.

The offices of the bank remained the same as before, but a commercial office was opened on the street in the same building. The partners hired two tellers and bought a large used safe which they had installed in the interior of the back office. Within a month, they had several ranchers as clients and were doing a good foot-traffic.

Samuel had stayed in the upstairs bank office to handle the business of his original customers and some of the new ranch accounts; Richard had his office in the street-side storefront. Richard and Samuel were a good fit as partners, and Samuel felt confident enough in the arrangement to take his granddaughter Ruth to New York so she could be married. Richard expected him to be gone a month.

While Samuel was gone, Richard worked long hours. Besides the days he was in the public area of the bank, he usually spent an hour or two in the evenings with clients in the bank's upper office.

About three weeks after Samuel left, a wiry man of indeterminate years came into the bank just as Richard was closing the public area. He asked Richard if he could talk to him about a loan and asked for an appointment. The man's name was Tim Norton, and he had a ranch near Beaumont, Texas.

Richard was supposed to have dinner with Jeremy and something in the back of his mind told Richard he might want to ask Tim Norton to go with him. The two men walked the few blocks to the restaurant where Jeremy and Richard were going to meet.

Jeremy was surprised to see Tim. They had met a few years before when both men had brought some horses to the auction in Houston. Aside from an exchange of names and a handshake, the men were strangers. Jeremy looked at Richard and wondered what had prompted him to add the man as a guest for dinner.

The meal was good, the food plentiful, and the steaks well-cooked. Conversation was confined to ranching, families, and the weather. When the waiter brought the coffee, Richard asked Tim if he would like to talk about his loan request in front of Jeremy or if he still needed the appointment.

Jeremy understood why Tim was at dinner with them when Richard mentioned Tim was looking for a loan. Not being familiar with the area around Beaumont, Richard probably wanted Jeremy to help him with the discussion. Tim talked about his reasons for the loan.

Some areas of Texas were in the beginnings of a drought and Tim's ranch, like Jeremy's big ranch in south-central Texas, was starting to feel the effects. Jeremy had told Richard about the beginning effects of the drought just before Samuel left for New York, but at his ranch the river which ran through the property was helping his sons, who ran the ranch for him, stave off the kind of problems Tim was having. While Tim's ranch had a couple of spring-fed stock ponds on it, there was no river or live water.

Tim was looking to improve his herd with a Herford bull. The calves would be beefier, bring a better price, and he wouldn't need as many to make the ranch even more profitable. Instead of running several hundred cows to get a bunch of calves that needed more water, he could run less cow and calf units and get meatier stock to take to market. Jeremy understood the man's thinking, but he did have a problem with the idea of the Herford bull. When Richard first met him, Jeremy had given him a long lecture about the problems with the short, stocky calves that some ranchers were breeding with bulls like the Herford. The problems with birthing them, their stamina over the rough terrain, foraging, and the short horns were no match for the local predators. Jeremy talked to Tim for a good hour about the subject in an attempt to dissuade him from going that route with his stock.

Tim, however, did not see another solution. He had to make the ranch pay, but he needed water. Jeremy asked him about digging wells, but Tim was way ahead of him. "Jeremy, the last three wells they dug had water, but it weren't fit to drink and the cows wouldn't go near it."

Two days later, against Jeremy's advice, Richard decided to make the loan to Tim Norton to buy the bull. The paperwork was drawn up and within six weeks, a sturdy, big bull arrived by train and Tim was at the station to claim his ranch's savior.

When Samuel returned, Richard sat with him and went over all of the business done in his absence. The loan to Tim Norton was the only one Samuel questioned. The other business was very much to the partner's liking, but not the loan for the bull. Still, Samuel understood the younger man needed to have a bad loan at least once if he was going to learn to be more conservative and cautious in the future.

Just as Jeremy and Samuel feared, Tim Norton was about to default. The drought deepened and fewer calves could be kept with the amount of water the stock ponds had produced the previous year. Now, even the springs were drying up.

Tim came to see Richard to ask for an extension of his time. Richard said he would have to discuss it with his partner, but Samuel was not willing to extend the loan.

That evening, Tim and Richard had dinner and Richard told him the bad news. Tim, however, had a counter offer. He offered to sell a piece of his ranch to the bank to cover the loan. Richard did not think Samuel would consider it was a fair trade, but Richard decided to take the chance on Tim again.

This time, the business was handled outside of the bank. Richard told Samuel what he was doing, and was told he was free to do what he wished with his own money, just as long as the bank was paid for the loan. The lawyer drew up the papers and Richard bought the land from Tim who used the money to pay the bank. As Richard read the documents, he noticed the phrase "mineral rights" had been added to the description of what he was buying.

The lawyer, a Boston-trained attorney, told Richard it was something he had learned when he read law. "It probably doesn't mean anything, but I was told to put it in any land contracts I did."

For the rest of Richard's life—well, at least until the turn of the century—it was just a thousand acres of east Texas land which, with no water, had little chance of ever being worth anything. Tim still grazed his cattle on the land and for this; he paid Richard a fee when he had the money available. Richard did get out to the see the land once and it was unremarkable as land went. In fact, in 1879, when he was just going on thirty years old, he had almost forgotten about buying it. After the oil strike in 1901, the phrase, "mineral rights" began to payoff, and he was glad it was in the contract. Richard had learned an important lesson, and for the next two years he spent long hours building up the bank with Samuel. There were some bad loans, but it was more to do with the spreading drought and the drop in the cattle market. Cattle was no longer "king" as many had touted and just like "king cotton," cattle's day had come and gone. The big operations with plenty of live water or deep spring–fed stock ponds were able to survive. Many of the men who ran these spreads had put away for a down period by tightening their belts, both by saving their capital, and husbanding their water.

———— ◈ ————

1881

Two years after the partnership was formed, the bank was doing a good, steady business. Richard took a trip to New York to make some contacts with the city's moneymen and, while he was there, was fitted with a pair of glasses, which helped with his sight. The men in London started to lose interest in their American investments as the drought expanded over all of Texas and the majority of the West. They pulled out all of their money, but Samuel and Richard were able to step in and the ranchers they served were happier with American money anyway.

Jeremy's youngest son brought his wife to the "Lazy H," after which Abbey, Jeremy's wife, thought it would be a good time to move to town. With much cajoling, Jeremy took a house west of the growing city, not far from the property Richard had bought a few years before.

Richard still rented in town. He had left Miss Abigail Johnson's boarding house and moved his meager belongings to an apartment above a store near the bank. He did have an open invitation to dinner at Jeremy's, and Miss Lucy was always pleased when he accepted.

Jeremy wasn't suited to city life and spent his days at the Cattlemen's Club talking cows and ranching and, on a few occasions, accepted invitations to visit other men's ranches. Abbey knew it was hard on him, but Doc Harris was also worried about her husband's health—and the doctor was in Houston, not on the ranch.

1883

Doc Harris married Red's sister, Elbeth, and the couple had just had a redheaded little girl whom everyone was sure would grow up to break a lot of hearts. The couple lived near Abbey, and they were also frequent visitors at the Higgin's home.

Red gave his sister away to Doc Harris on a Sunday and got on the train to Fort Worth the next day. Three weeks later the newlyweds, Red and his wife, arrived by wagon to the Chadwick ranch. Red had married Miss Millie Nelson, daughter of George Nelson, who owned the Buckle R over near the panhandle. She was a rancher's daughter and understood ranch life.

When Red handed his bride down from the wagon, they made an odd couple. She was tiny to his big frame and had very delicate-looking hands and feet as well as a wispy waist. Anyone looking at her would think she could break in the slightest breeze, but once they got to know her, they found she had a backbone and a will of steel.

Red had been courting Miss Millie for almost three years, but until his sister was married, he couldn't ask her to wed. With Elbeth's wedding, it was time to bring his bride into the home. Elbeth was happy for him, and Red was pleased it had all worked out for them both. The pressure, however, on Richard to settle down, was growing.

———◄((◉))►———

Just before his thirty-third birthday, he commissioned a surveyor to plot his land. The official plat showed he owned just over thirty-seven acres. He marked off some sections on the map the man made and asked him to go back to the property and plot the changes.

The shape of the land made it possible for Richard to cut an easement for a street to run near the top edge of his property. On the north side of the easement and running along the bayou, with just under thirty acres, he would build his house. On the other side of the "street" was a little more than seven acres. Richard took the papers to the city/ county land office and filed his revised plat and deeds. The seven acres would be his contribution to establishing an Anglican church along his road.

For the last year, a group of about twenty had been attending a prayer service in the Methodist church after regular services were finished. The group, mostly couples, was all Anglican and, like Richard, had a goal of having their own church. This land would be his part in seeing that the church would be built. Some of the couples had children, there were some older people, and then there were the younger men. It was a nice start for a church, and it was something Richard wanted to push forward.

Richard also wanted to have a church building where he could be married. A letter to his brother, the Reverend Edgar Farr, helped him locate a suitably trained Anglican priest to become the first Rector of the new church. Before the priest could be hired, however, a Vestry was elected from the church group. Three men, Richard among them, were chosen for the first three-year term. A letter was sent to the Reverend Sylas Martine, inviting him to visit with the hopes he would be hired to be the priest at the church. During the first meeting of the Vestry, two names were proposed for the church and a vote called of all the members. The overwhelming vote was for the church to be called St. John's. Richard also started the build on his own home. He and Miss Lucy had reached an "understanding" that once the house was finished, there would be an official engagement. The man he had bought the property from had given him some plans, which had been drawn up by an architect in New York, but Richard didn't like them and worked with a man in Houston to find a design he preferred.

Originally, Richard had thought about building a home similar to Farr Cottage, but this would have been next to impossible on the budget he had set. The Cottage evolved over hundreds of years and was much larger than the original building with additions made by various members of the family down through the generations. He wanted a house with clean lines and of a single style, not a jumble of architecture like the Cottage.

On a break during one term while he was at Oxford, Richard had visited a school friend whose family lived in something he liked, and it was what he wanted. The Regency had been a stylish era, and the friend's house was built during its height. Working with a local man, a similar house would include three floors, eight bedrooms, and servant's quarters. In addition, it would also have a stable and other outbuildings. The building itself would simply be a large square with eight bedrooms on the second floor. On the first floor there would be a parlor, study, dining room, day room, other public rooms, and a kitchen attached to the back. On top of the main structure would be attics and servant's quarters. The builder recommended some local tiles for the roof in place of the slate Richard had seen on his friend's house in England. Other materials would be made of local variations, but when it was complete, he knew the home would be a comfortable place for his bride and their future children.

Construction on the church was progressing. Money was being solicited from the congregation, which had now grown to more than forty-five. A two-room house had been built for the new Vicar. Services took place outside, but if the weather was nasty, they were held in the big room of the house. Richard and the rest of the Vestry members spent much of their time talking to new people about joining the church, and the shell of the church building was almost complete.

———◉———

1884

The day work was finished on his new house, Richard rode to Jeremy's place so he could formally ask Miss Lucy to be his wife. Abbey and Jeremy made the engagement a big party with the doctor and Elbeth, Solomon and his new wife, Sarah, and a few of the people Richard knew from his work at the bank.

Miss Lucy and Abbey had been preparing for the event for quite some time and it was a well-attended affair. More than fifty people came, and it was the basis of the guest list for the wedding. Lucy's mother would come for the marriage and other friends and family would also travel for the wedding, but the engagement party just included the local community.

Richard had consulted with Lucy about the furnishings for the house and had all but handed over the task to Abbey and Lucy. He had to admit, their taste in furnishings and appointments to the house were wonderful. All he had to do was move in his clothes and put his horse in the barn and he could begin living in his own home.

Abbey and Lucy had also been preparing for the wedding. A trousseau of clothes, linens, and other items had been gathered and added to over the preceding years. Abbey had helped Lucy with stitching and embroidery, knitting, and tatting of lace. A large assortment of doilies, anti-massacres, and table linens, occupied almost two chests.

Richard and Lucy's wedding day was a big event. Carriages lined the lane to the small, newly finished church, Miss Lucy carried a bouquet of bluebells, and the church alter was adorned with the same flowers. By the time the bride entered the sanctuary, there was standing room only. A cool, late April breeze helped to keep the guests comfortable during the service.

Jeremy had given the bride away and the reception was held at his home. Lucy's mother and a younger sister had attended, and Abbey had outdone herself putting the event together. A cold lunch was served on the lawn, and a group of musicians played as the guests visited and chatted about everything from the weather to the bride's lovely yellow gown. Toasts were made to the new couple and when all was finished, the bride and groom left for their new home. Richard and Lucy spent their wedding night in Houston, but boarded a train for New Orleans the next morning. Unlike many honeymoons of the day, theirs would be no longer than two weeks. Richard needed to return to the bank and couldn't be gone as long as Lucy might have liked.

＊＊＊

Richard was given a chance to buy Solomon's share of the bank and in 1890, the name was changed to Farr's Bank. By the end of the century, air-conditioning was being made available for installation in office buildings. Richard also had it put in the family home by the Bayou. The new bank building that Richard built in downtown Houston had six floors, an elevator, and was fully "cooled."

＊＊＊

1885

Time passed quickly for the young couple. Lucy and Richard had two children, Annis and Avery. Annis was the oldest by a mere three minutes and took it as a sign she needed to watch over her "little" brother. Avery and Annis both attended the church school at St. John's before Avery was sent to boarding school.

Avery Arthur Farr had the same knack for numbers his father had shown when he was a young man. The instructors at the boarding school he attended in Groton, Massachusetts, found him to be a fine, all-around student with a penchant for the church.

The Reverend Sylas Marine had recommended the new school at Groton because it was affiliated with the Anglican Communion, but also because the headmaster was someone he knew personally. Father Marine was very much aware Richard wanted Avery to follow him in the banking business. A good education, both in the classics and religion, would give the boy a moral compass that would run as true as the one Avery's own father had shown. Annis also attended school beyond the primary classes given at St. John's. Miss Evangeline Turner's school for young ladies was where most of the girls from her mother and father's friends sent their children. Miss Lucy taught her what she needed to know as far as fine needlework, the running of a house, and she had instilled in her a sense of purpose as a wife; but the school taught her music, singing, some Spanish and Latin, and deportment. The goal of each of the girls was to have a "presentation" party at the time of their graduation.

Much like the "season" or being presented at court Richard had experienced when he was a young man in London, there was no court of royals to whom these girls could be introduced. Instead, they were made known to society, dressed in their best finery, and were proclaimed, by their families, to be available to be courted.

1905

Several of the families had parties for their daughters after the "coming out" party all of the girls attended. There were a number of reasons for the extra show; for some it was simply a way to let the community see their wealth. For others, it was to give a plain daughter a venue where she could shine brighter than her fellow debutantes. Annis's family choose not to have a separate event, but they did allow her to attend the other girl's parties as long as her brother, Avery, was her escort. It was at one of these parties, given during one of Avery's school breaks from Harvard, when Avery met the girl he would later marry.

Interlude In London

Present Day

Melody closed the file and laid it with the others, on which she had spent the last thirteen weeks working. The letters, diary entries, and jottings about her great-great grandfather had consumed her time and attention since the day her guardian had started her on this slice of the Farr family history. Now, it was finished—well, mostly. There were still some questions she had for Sir Arthur, but she wouldn't interrupt him until he finished his current task.

In the beginning, Melody would stop and ask each time she came upon something which was unclear. However, her cousin soon let her know that was not how he wanted them to work together. They would spend long hours, each at their own desks, working on their individual projects, and not a word would pass between them. Lunch would be brought in on trays and would be eaten while they worked.

Earlier in the afternoon, Nedda would come in to light the fire and close the curtains against the gathering chill. The soft summer days since Melody's arrival at Farr Cottage had turned to fall. The forests, which stood on the estate's property, were turning to colors of red, yellow, gold, and orange.

Melody was missing her mother. This was the time of year they would have normally been busy preparing for Thanksgiving, working on Christmas cards and gift lists, and attending to projects their church had for the holidays. Both women would help serve lunch to the homeless at the church on Thanksgiving Day, and boxes of essentials would go with each person who had come to eat. Hats and scarves had been knitted by members of one of the ministry groups and added to the blanket, gloves, and warm socks in the boxes.

Livia Paxton, wife of the Reverend Charles Paxton, had enlisted Melody's help with the ladies of the local church to make baskets of goodies for some of the troops still serving in Afghanistan, but in Britain, any homeless were cared for by the government. She attended Sunday and Wednesday evening services, but the variety of activities in this church was far below that to which she was accustomed.

Melody pushed the keyboard drawer on the desk away from her. Sir Arthur had surprised her one day with a new, larger desk and a computer. She had been using her own laptop, but after the first two weeks, her guardian acknowledged the efficiency of the computer and the fact it would make things much easier. Now, Melody's own machine was in her room for late night e-mails with her girlfriend in Houston, and the machine on her desk was only used for work.

A printer-scanner unit had been ordered but had not yet arrived. Melody wanted to add the photos she had found to the narrative she had written. In her Houston home, there were many more she would contribute to the work, but it would be sometime in the future before this could happen. She had never gone through any of the papers, stacks of old letters, or photos in the library at home, but now she looked forward to a journey of discovery.

Arthur realized the soft click of the computer keyboard had stopped. He put down his pen, closed his book, and pushed his chair back. "Have you finished for the day? There is an hour or more of time before we have to dress for dinner. Is something wrong?"

"No, sir, the work on this part of the family is finished." Melody said, "but, well, I do have some questions for you."

Sir Arthur stood and took a book off the shelf behind his desk. "We can talk about the questions you have at dinner. If you want, take the extra time for yourself, and I'll see you in the lounge at the regular time."

Melody got up and took her sweater from the back of her desk chair. "Thank you. I think a long, hot bath will be a wonderful treat today. I'll see you at five thirty."

Every evening since her guardian had arrived, they had followed the same schedule. If guests were coming for dinner, the time to meet in the lounge was still 5:30, but guests were invited to arrive at 6 p.m. with dinner at 6:30. Only on Wednesday evenings, when Melody went to prayer services at the church, did the program change. On those nights, Melody and her cousin would eat when they returned from services, and then have coffee and brandy in the lounge.

Both Melody and Sir Arthur were normally immersed in their work, and guests for dinner were a rarity. The Paxtons would come every other week and after the first month, even Lord Alfred was welcomed. A couple of times, business associates of her guardian would come for dinner, but nothing was ever said in Melody's presence about the kind of "business" in which her cousin was engaged. Since the men never brought their wives with them, she was not required or requested to sit and have coffee with them while they had drinks in the study with Lord Arthur.

Melody liked Farr Cottage and, after the first month or so, began to feel at home. It took a direct request from her to her cousin to have a full tour, but so little of the house was in use; the majority of the rooms simply remained closed.

It also took some time to settle on what Melody would call her guardian. She didn't feel comfortable just calling him Arthur, but Lord Arthur, Sir Arthur, or Viscount of Gibbons were so formal it seemed clunky to her American sensibilities. It was agreed Melody would call him simply sir while they were working, or Cousin Arthur when outside of work hours.

As she walked down the corridor to her room, the five closed doors which lined the hallway were a testament to the emptiness of Farr Cottage. There was also the long passageway, which led to her cousin's room, a place she had never ventured except the one time during her tour of the house. On the opposite side of the house, another long hall led to its own set of rooms.

Farr Cottage

All of the rooms on the Cottage's first floor were public, except of course, for the kitchen, pantry, and butler's pantry area. She and her cousin worked in the library, but there was also a study just off the library. In addition, a formal living room was used when guests were entertained and during the evening's "before dinner drink." Next to the formal living room was a day room, lined on one wall with floor to ceiling windows, which was used for those times when Sir Arthur and Melody weren't working. The dining room was large, but not as huge as the one in her Houston home. Beside the dining room was a small breakfast room, which, like the day room, had windows that looked out over the lawn to the forest.

The outside of the house was a mishmash of styles that were a testament to the long history of the Cottage. Stone and brick were used for the exterior and with the installation of plumbing and electricity over various renovations; the interior was covered with oak paneling, plaster, or in the older parts, tapestries. During Victorian times, a conservatory was added and the gardens replanted. However, the gardens were tended on an irregular basis and had fallen into a sad state.

A long, hot bath was just the thing to help her relax. Melody was the first to admit she did some of her best thinking in the bath or shower. She may feel at home in Farr Cottage, but she still longed to return to her home in Houston. Her work on her family's past had pushed the historian in her to want to study the photos, letters, and other papers in the library at home. There were things missing, and Melody was sure they could be found there. As much as the work fascinated her, she wanted to go home. Melody had never had many friends, but the ones she did have she missed, and just the feel of her own room in the family home called to her. Tonight at dinner, she would tell her cousin she wanted to go home.

The terms of the will did not prevent her from living in Houston. It was her guardian's wish she be in his house, where he could watch over her, but she was almost twenty-nine. She could look after herself. Maybe she could even be back home in time for Thanksgiving and Christmas. The idea continued to form as she dressed for dinner.

The burgundy red charmeuse silk slipped over her figure and hugged her in all the right places. A velvet jacket in a matching color would help ward off a chill. She was ready to go down to have her before dinner whiskey and dine with her guardian. Melody would tell her cousin at dinner she would be going to Houston for the holidays with the intention of staying on to study the contents of the home library.

Sir Arthur stood near the drinks cart when Melody walked in the room, and he handed her a glass of whiskey just the way she liked it. Neither of them took ice in their drinks, and while Sir Arthur drank his scotch neat, she always had water in hers. He never asked her what she wanted and made it the very same way each time out of habit.

From the corner of his eye, he watched as Melody took a sip of her drink and sat in the little ladies' chair in front of the fire. She was a fine-looking thing and had the grace of movement, which reminded him of liquid gold. In the time he had spent working with her, he found her to be quite modest and seemingly unaware just how lovely she was.

Sir Arthur frowned. Hmm, and this was the problem. What to do with her. He worried about her as if she was a teenager with no idea of what she wanted. Melody had never talked to him about any desires to find a husband or even wanting to look for one. His ward should marry but it had to be the right person. Alfred had been sniffing around her since the day after she arrived, but he wasn't anyone Arthur could even consider. No, it might be he would have to look at suitable mates. With her bloodline, he could probably make a good match for her. The problem: would she see it his way or think he was meddling in something she might consider personal?

"Melody, I have to go to Paris on business. Before leaving for the continent however, I shall spend a few days in London. Would you like to go with me before you begin the next part of your work?"

Melody's eyes lit up. "Oh yes, I would love to go to Paris!" Her guardian set his drink on the small table at his elbow. "No, my dear, I am not asking you to go to Paris, just to London for a few days. Would you like to go?"

Melody's hopes were only slightly deflated; Paris had sounded so wonderful, but she would take London and look forward to seeing Paris in the future. "Yes, Cousin Arthur, I'd love to go to London. When?"

Arthur was happy he had gotten that in order. "We can take the noon train tomorrow. Pack for, oh, three, maybe four days. Umm, and we shall probably eat out one evening so make sure you have the proper clothes."

"Thank you, I will. There is something I wanted to ask you—or really, tell you—this evening. I, uh, well ..."

Arthur watched the girl trying to put her thoughts into words. Best to stop this before it got started. "Melody, we are about to go into dinner. Perhaps you should tell me after we eat, over coffee. How's that? Hmm? It will give you time to decide what you want to say."

Melody looked down, perhaps now was not the time to announce her decision to leave. She watched her cousin as a frown again creased his forehead. Whatever he had on his mind was weighing on him.

Nedda was a fine cook, and dinner was superb. Melody and her guardian did not care much for fancy fair but did like variety and spice. Although the discussion over dinner was not about Melody's desire to return home to Houston, it did cover some of her questions.

"Cousin Arthur, you said you would let me ask you some things about the work I have just done," Melody started. "Do you mind if I ask them now?"

Her cousin put his fork down and took a sip from his wineglass. "I don't like to talk about work during a meal, but I did promise. Go ahead, ask your questions."

Melody started down her mental list. "Why do they call this house Farr Cottage? Was it simply taken from the name of the family?"

Arthur smiled; this story would take some time. "Our family goes back to before the Conquest. At the time, many names were simply first names with 'son of' as a way to identify who a person was. So for example, Joffrey son of Harold, son of Godwin. No last names, just a linage. We are an Old Saxon family, and this was how our king knew us." Arthur took another sip of his wine and then continued, "Our family had always been loyal knights to their kings. When the king would travel, he constantly had a large entourage of knights, courtiers, ladies, and servants. They would go from one house to another and stay for days or weeks. It took a lot of room to house them all, and the amount of food and victuals they used could break even the wealthiest knight."

"Well, each time the king would talk about visiting Joffrey, son of Harold, son of Godwin, our ancestor would tell him he had 'but a small cottage and that it is very far' to visit. It was the king who, probably, as a joke, started calling him Joffrey Farr—Farr being the old English spelling of *far*. And, when a king finally did visit 'Farr Cottage,' he found it to be a substantial stone house, much more than a cottage of the day."

"It was a good thing the kings didn't visit very often. The first trip put the family in a crofter's cottage in order to have enough room to accommodate the king's retinue in the 'cottage.' Before the next royal visit, Farr Cottage was expanded for the comfort of the family." Melody's cousin turned to her, "So does this answer your question? Do you have more, or can we eat our fruit in peace?"

Melody pressed on, "What about the title Viscount of Gibbons? Where does it come in?"

Arthur had an apple in his hand and continued to peel it while he talked. "The title came much later. There had been a Viscount of Gibbons, but during the English Civil War, the Viscount's family sided with the Roundheads against the Royalists of the true king. In the course of the Restoration, Charles II rewarded families who had stayed loyal to the Crown or had done them some service in their absence with titles. Several families claimed it was in retaliation and went against the agreement made which facilitated the Restoration, but others saw them as being traitors to the royal family. It was all a big storm in a teacup until the titles were affirmed during the reigns of William and Mary."

Finished with his fruit, Arthur laid his napkin beside his plate and the meal was over. He held the chair for his ward, and they both retired to the lounge for coffee and brandy.

Melody pressed on with her questions, "You said something about performing a service to the Crown. What was it that would be worth a Viscount?"

Arthur took the brandy snifter from Melody's hand. "Here, come with me. I want to show you something."

Melody was led up the stairs to the second floor, down the corridor past where her room was located, and into the long hall branching off on the opposite end from the one where Arthur had his rooms. Her guardian turned on a light, which illuminated the hall. Six closed doors were on either side of the passageway.

At the end, a full-sized painting could be seen. Arthur flipped a switch next to the picture, and a light bathed the family portrait. There, on the canvas, was a life-size depiction of a father and mother with sons, daughters, and their pets.

Arthur pointed to the family. "So, tell me what you see. You're a trained historian, look for clues to the time period and any elements which might jump out at you."

Melody stepped up to the painting and looked carefully. The dress of the people was in the style of the mid-1600s, the father was seated with his wife standing slightly back and to the side. The oldest boy stood next to the father and the other children, boys and girls, were seated around the feet of their father and mother. One of the small girls held a doll, and two boys had a dog between them. Farr Cottage was used as a backdrop in the fashion of a Dobson painting. Melody looked at her cousin. "The dog, is it a Cavalier King Charles Spaniel?"

Arthur smiled. "Very good! It certainly is. King Charles even had his two favorite dogs hidden in his robes when he was beheaded. And, as his son, the future Charles II and his mother fled to France, some of his family stopped here on their way. The Roundheads were after them and in the interests of traveling light, they left two of his dogs here." Arthur pointed at the dog. "And this is one of them."

Melody turned to her guardian. "Amazing, but you said there were two dogs. Where is the other?"

"Oh, yes, there were two, but according to the notes left about this painting, the other dog had puppies and was not allowed in the

Anita D. Boseman

room where the artist was working. Now, do you notice anything else about the picture?"

Melody again scrutinized the subjects but drew a blank. She then looked at the way the painter showed Farr Cottage. It seemed smaller in the painting, but maybe it was the perspective. She took a chance on this being the situation. "Farr Cottage looks much smaller." She looked back at her cousin. "It's the Cottage, right?"

Arthur chuckled. The girl had a good eye and was observant. He would have to remember this before he told her about his own business. "Yes, it is the Cottage. The original stone Cottage is within the main structure and, except for some places in the floor, it is hard to determine exactly where it is. The Cottage in the time of the Norman invasion was much smaller than it is today. In fact, it was just after this was painted that the Cottage was expanded yet again. Then it was enlarged after the Restoration, during the Regency, and for the last time during the reign of Victoria."

Arthur looked up at the ceiling and back down at Melody. He shrugged. "I suppose it's why the house is such a hodgepodge of styles." His cousin turned off the light over the picture and they left to return to the lounge.

Melody took two replacement cups from the coffee tray and made each of them a fresh, hot cup. They had been gone long enough that the coffee left in the fine china cups was cold and unappetizing. While she worked, Melody thought it would be a good time to bring up her intentions of going home. "Cousin Arthur, before dinner you said I could speak to you about something after we ate. Well, as much as I've enjoyed being here, working on the family history, and meeting everyone, I want to go home." She hurried on before her guardian could comment. "This time of year was always very special for my mother and me. It will soon be Thanksgiving in America, and I want to spend Christmas in my own home. So, after we return from London, well, it would be a good time to leave."

Arthur was surprised. He thought she was settling in to a life in Farr Cottage. Granted, the first week was rocky, but the problem had straightened out. He'd had a word with Nedda who then fixed her attitude toward Melody. He had even let that scoundrel Alfred come

102

for dinner a few times to make her happy. Now this? He couldn't stop her from leaving, but he wanted her to come back. This was a problem he didn't need.

Melody watched her cousin's face and looked for any body language, which would tell her about his response to what she had just told him. He was difficult to read, but he didn't look happy. The initial reaction was shock, but he quickly covered his expression with his "worried" look. Melody, however, had not really expected her Cousin Arthur to be happy about her decision.

Arthur gathered his thoughts and armored his outward appearance. "Melody, my dear, perhaps a trip back to Houston would be a good idea. You've said there are items which would add to the work you have already done, and it would also give you a chance to visit friends. Enjoy your holidays, and then we can expect you back, oh, let's say, in the second week of January."

As if Melody had said nothing more unsettling than a comment on the weather, he changed the subject. "It's getting late and tomorrow will be a busy day. I suggest you go to bed and Nedda will pack your things in the morning. We leave on the noon train." He turned back to his brandy. "Pleasant dreams."

Melody had expected more emotion from her cousin, but his way of treating the announcement that she would return to Houston was disconcerting to her. She set her cup and saucer on the tray before standing to leave the room. "Good night, cousin. May you also have pleasant dreams."

Before Arthur could respond, she had turned and left. The fire in the lounge had kept the room at a comfortable temperature, but the rest of the house was decidedly chilly. She just hoped a lit fire would warm her room.

Early the next morning, while Melody was finishing her bath, Nedda came to pack the suitcases. John had done the same for Cousin Arthur, and after a hearty breakfast, Melody and he went to the library to get a few hours' work accomplished before the train. Nothing much was said, and no reference was made to Melody's plans to return to Houston.

The porter took their bags from the train and put them in the trunk of a black taxi· (A Black Cab is a specific designation for a London hackney-carriage of distinctive design. The drivers have to pass a test call "The Knowledge" to show they have intimate knowledge of the geography of London streets, important buildings, can plan alternate routes in cases of congestion, etc.)

Melody and her cousin settled into the back seat while the cabbie found his way to the address he'd been given. After the peace of the village, London was noisy. Even Houston, as big as it was, had never been this loud to Melody unless it was barbeque cook-off time at the rodeo.

Nevertheless, she looked out the window, at the people and the buildings, as they sped past. Before long, however, the taxi pulled onto a short street with white row houses on each side. Each looked like the other and stood three or four stories tall. Halfway down the street, a narrow side street cut between the houses. The cab slowed and stopped before one of the houses next to the short alley.

Arthur paid the cabbie and opened the front door to the house on the end. The driver put the suitcases in the foyer while Melody looked up and down the street. For all the hustle and bustle of the city, this little street was very quiet, almost another world.

Arthur called to her to come inside, and she entered a large foyer. A staircase ran up one side of the room and beyond it, a door looked into a dining room. Her cousin flipped a switch and the lights came on. A bow window, which looked out onto the street, had been the only light, but now Melody could see the rest of the entryway.

An ornate chandelier hung from a sturdy chain that was fastened into the ceiling two floors above. Around the room, wall sconces splashed light onto walls covered in very old-fashioned flocked wallpaper with burgundy and cream stripes. Paintings hung around the room and up the wall on the stairs. A wainscoting of aged wood, probably oak, was in need of a dusting and oiling.

Next to the door, an elaborate umbrella stand stood half-filled. A table with a tarnished silver dish waited to receive calling cards from visitors who never came. Near it was an empty vase with a faded water stain, which should have held fresh flowers to greet both homeowners and visitors alike. The whole room looked old and tired.

Arthur opened a hidden door in the paneling under the stairs and simply said, "kitchen." Melody had been a fan of the *Upstairs, Downstairs* series shown on American television in the 1970s and available on her ROKU player. It was the first time she had seen a "below stairs" door, which would take servants to the kitchen area of a townhouse. In Houston, the houses had bigger footprints, and the kitchen and servant's quarters were hidden in different ways.

Arthur took the suitcases and told Melody to follow him. He headed up the stairs, but instead of stopping on the next floor, he continued up to the floor above. He walked to a door, set the cases down, and opened it. "This is your room. I will bring the rest of the things up in a few minutes."

Melody looked inside and with only a sliver of light sneaking between the closed curtains, she could not make out much of the interior. She felt for the light switch and found it near the backside of the door. The overhead light was weak, but once she had pulled back the curtains, the room perked up with sunny yellow wallpaper and a chintz bedapread and window coverings. The furniture was a light-colored wood that had the style of the 1920s or art deco feel to them. The room also had an attached bath, but it wasn't nearly as nice as the one in Farr Cottage.

At a knock on the door, she turned to see her cousin with the suit bag in his hand. "I'll put this in the closet and you can get unpacked. We should meet downstairs in, oh, say, an hour. One of your dark suits would be nice. We will go have a tea and do a bit of visiting. Some old friends of the family want to meet you."

Before she could say anything, she could hear him walking back down the hall. Melody went to the door and saw him disappear into a room at the opposite end of the corridor. She moved back into the room, closed the door, and started putting things away.

Dressed in a conservative navy suit with a white silk blouse, Melody met her cousin near the front door. He watched her as she descended the stairs and again marveled at her slender ankles. The heels she wore with the ensemble gave her a leggy look that he found quite appealing.

"Before we go," Arthur said, "I will show you the rest of this floor." He walked to the wall opposite the stairway and slid the double pocket doors open. The flip of a light switch illuminated a formal sitting room much larger than Melody had expected.

The furnishings were all dark wood Victorian pieces, which looked original to the period. The room, like most done in the style, seemed to have an overabundance of everything. Chairs, side tables, camel-backed sofas, and large curio cabinets would make it hard to move around. Without saying anything, Arthur backed out of the room, turned off the light, and slid the doors closed.

"Hmmm. A bit over filled for my tastes too but, in its day, quite the fashionable salon. My great-grandmother's family owned the house next door to ours. When she married, the two houses were literally joined. The front door on this part of the house does not open because it was blocked with the building of this room. The bow window in the sitting room was the only thing they kept. They also removed the stairs and"—pointing to the ones Melody had just walked down—"made these the only ones, besides the backstairs, to go to the upper floors."

Arthur continued, "No one, at that time, wanted to change the outside of the houses, but the insides were almost completely done over. Changing the outsides of these buildings is no longer allowed. Below us, there is a large kitchen, enough quarters for all of the servants, and storage for food as well as a sizeable wine cellar." He walked to the back of the foyer and slid open the doors Melody had seen were partially open when she first came in.

A long, highly polished dining table and chairs graced the room. Seating for twenty people made this dining room almost as large as the one in her house in Houston. Two small chandeliers, each one identical to the one in the foyer, hung over the table. A large fireplace filled one wall and a buffet sat on the opposite wall. Several pieces of slightly tarnished silver sat under clear covers on the buffet and on the table. The room appeared to be unused and forgotten.

On the last wall, Arthur slid pocket doors, which led into a billiard/game room also furnished with Victorian pieces. "After dinner, the ladies would sit in the salon with coffee, and the men would come in here for cigars, brandy, and 'men's talk.' My great-grandparents did a lot of entertaining and they needed all this space. I only use the house when I'm in London. It's easier than a hotel."

Melody started to say something, but Arthur looked over to her. "It's time for us to leave. Just let me shut these doors and we can go."

Arthur and Melody left by the front door. She was surprised to see there was no taxi. Her cousin directed her to the short, narrow street next to the house. "It's just back here. When everyone had a carriage, they had to have a place to store them, to stable the horses, and to house the coachman as well as possibly a groom. When the two houses were joined, the mews in the back were also joined. I keep a car in one side, but the other side was changed into a very nice apartment. The old coachman's quarters above the garage where the car stays were also made into a small flat, and the lady who used to be the cook in the house lives there."

The outside of the mews buildings had been painted white. A garage door opened easily and beside that door was another that must have led to the flat above the garage. Arthur pushed a door chime that was beside it. A few moments later, an elderly lady in a corduroy skirt and knitting set opened the door.

"Sir Arthur, why didn't you call ahead? I could have had the house open for you. And who is this lovely girl?" Melody blushed slightly at the compliment.

"Melody, this is Mrs. Jones. She used to work here, but retired when my late mother and father closed the house." He turned to

Mrs. Jones. "Melody Farr is my cousin from America. She is my ward and will be with us for another couple of years. Her great-great grandfather was Richard Farr."

The woman looked Melody up and down. "Hmmm, yes, I can see the family resemblance." Mrs. Jones turned her attention back to Cousin Arthur. "Will you be in London long? Would you like me to get my niece in to help while you are here?"

Arthur nodded. "Yes, please, we will probably go at the end of the week, but in case we do have visitors, I suppose we should have someone in the house. Call Angie, but tell her it is only for the week. And do you feel up to doing a breakfast or lunch here and there?"

"Oh, Sir Arthur, for the family? Of course. Is there anything in particular, or just the usual?"

Arthur shook his head. "Whatever you do will be fine. Call round to the market and have them deliver what you need. We will be back later. See you in the morning."

Mrs. Jones smiled and retreated behind the door to her home. Arthur pulled out the car and Melody got in. The car was old, but comfortable. She guessed it was a late 50s or early 60s Jaguar.

Melody ran her hand over the fine leather of the seat and admired the polished wood on the dashboard. Arthur saw her admiring his car. "It's a 1955 MK1, 2.4. Saloon. Grandfather bought it when he and grandmother moved up to London. It was the first new car they felt like buying after the war was over. It's always been in London and has a ridiculously low number of miles on the clock. I've had people offer to buy it, but it's just too full of memories. Father proposed to mother in this car."

Melody was surprised. This was the first time since she had met her cousin where he actually seemed to have a reaction to something that seemed to come solely from the heart and not the head. She wasn't sure if it was just sentimentality for his family or if it was the car. Emotion was not normally apparent around Farr Cottage, with anyone, but especially not with her cousin.

Within a few minutes, Arthur pulled the car under the overhang of a stately old building. The architecture was art deco and the liveried doorman wore a top hat and overcoat. The man opened

Melody's door, and Arthur gave the keys to him to keep until they would be ready to leave.

Arthur steered Melody through the opened doors to the elevators. "The people we're coming to see were friends of my parents. Very old school, so please pardon them if they put their foot in it. He lost an older brother in the Battle of Britain and with taxes and such eating up their families estates, they no longer have their country house but live in London full time. If it gets too boring, let me know and we'll leave. Whatever you do, don't agree to stay for dinner. If they ask, we have other plans, and I wouldn't want to have any unpleasantness in front of them."

The elevator stopped on one of the upper floors and the two got out. Four apartment doors on the floor were arranged around the small elevator foyer. Arthur pushed the button for the chimes on door D-3, and the sound of the doorbell was audible. Very quickly, an older man and woman in their seventies opened the door.

Introductions were made and the lady, Hilly Marshall, showed them into the lounge. Hilly and her husband Frank immediately started talking. Melody just smiled and wondered if this was because they had few visitors or if they were really so glad to see her cousin Arthur. Frank immediately asked her if she wanted something to drink. Hilly reminded him she was putting tea on and to leave the whiskey for later.

Arthur did most of the talking, and Hilly soon got up to get the tea. Melody offered to help and followed her hostess to the kitchen. The men stayed behind and talked about Melody.

Frank handed Arthur a short drink. "I don't mind telling you, she's not what I had expected." The men sat near the fireplace and Frank continued, "When Hilly and I heard about you taking her in, well, we thought, at her age, there must be something wrong—looks, money, something, but, well, I don't know about the money, but she doesn't skimp in the looks department."

Arthur nodded. "She is well-educated, is fairly well off, and, as you have mentioned, not bad to look at. I'm supposed to watch over her for the next two years, until she reaches thirty. That is a provision in her late father's will. I had expected her to come, stay until she reached the majority as required for the estate, and then return to America. She has done some fine work on the family genealogy and will do more, but now she wants to go home, back to Houston."

Frank sipped his drink. "So, tell her she can't go or better yet, get her interested in someone here whom she won't want to leave. I'm surprised she's not married, but"—he looked off into the distance—"so much about things like that have gotten past me. Fix her up with someone."

Arthur frowned. "It's not like suitable young men are a two pence a dozen in the country. The only one around—and he is definitely not suitable—is young Alfred Oswin from Aldwin House. He has even taken to escorting her to church on Sundays and then on Wednesday evenings. Fortunately,

he is here in London, so he is not where she is most of the time. Other than that, I don't know who to introduce her to. I was hoping you and Hilly might have some ideas."

The women were just returning from the kitchen with the teacart, and the men watched in silence as they set it up. Arthur knew Frank would talk to Hilly, who would cast about among the young men they would term "suitable."

Less than an hour later, Arthur, and Melody had said their goodbyes and were back in the car. Expertly, Arthur maneuvered through the busy traffic. "I think we will have an early dinner this evening. We have plenty to do tomorrow, so you might want to get some rest. How does a nice curry sound? Or would you prefer some Chinese?"

Melody shrugged. "Whatever you think, I don't know the restaurants here, so you pick."

A short time later, Arthur pulled the car in front of a small café. The name on the big window told her she would be eating curry. An older Indian gentleman, who seemed to know her cousin quite well, met them at the entrance.

Then, seated at a table for two, Arthur did the ordering. Except for a couple of women and a lone man seated in booths, they were the only ones in the place. A lovely smell pervaded the restaurant, and it was then Melody realized she was hungry.

Their lunch had been earlier than usual because of the train and, although the tea at the Marshall's was nice, the small digestive biscuits served with it did not constitute a meal. A large plate of very mildly spiced curry with rice was set before her and a much hotter one served to her cousin. Melody could smell the heat from her guardian's dish.

Arthur had a small glass of beer with his meal and told Melody, "If the curry is too hot for you, it's best to drink beer or milk. Nothing else will slake the heat."

Melody just nodded. Her cousin must know she did not drink beer since she had told him this several times, but she did order a small glass of milk.

At the mews behind the house, Melody got out of the car before Arthur drove it into the garage. They walked down the small side street to the front of the house. Only moments after entering and closing the door behind them, the doorbell rang.

Arthur turned back to open the door, but told Melody she might want to go freshen up before having coffee. She was halfway across the foyer floor when her cousin answered the door. A familiar voice, that of Alfred, called to her and told her hello. Much to her cousin's consternation, Melody returned to the door.

"I called the house and they said you had both come up to London," he said to Melody, but to Arthur, "Nice to see you are letting her do some sightseeing. Am I too late to join the party for dinner?"

"Alfred," her cousin said sternly, "we have just returned from dinner and were going to have an early night. Melody was on her way to her room to change and freshen up."

Alfred turned his attention back to Melody. "Would you like to go dancing with me, or maybe have a drink at the pub? My local is just a couple streets over and an easy walk. What do you say?"

Melody looked over at her cousin. As hot as his curry had been, it didn't cause the kind of fire she saw in her guardian's eyes. She just didn't get the animosity between them. "Cousin Arthur has a busy schedule for tomorrow, so I don't think I want to go dancing."

Arthur beamed; maybe the girl was starting to see through young Alfred at last.

"But," Melody continued, "I would like to visit a local English pub." She turned to her cousin. "I really would like to go, please come with us."

Well, it was a partial victory, Arthur thought. At least she wouldn't be alone with Alfred, and she was taking his feelings into account. "Okay, we can go, but not for long. We do have a full day tomorrow. Go put some casual clothes on, a tweed would be good, and don't forget your overcoat. I don't want you getting sick." Melody hurried up the stairs.

Arthur turned to a grinning Alfred. "Rapscallion! Give us a few minutes and we'll be ready."

Alfred laughed. "Call me what you will, it doesn't bother. I'll be back in a few minutes and hope you're ready."

Less than fifteen minutes later, the two men, with Melody between them, were escorting her down the broad sidewalk to the cross street. There, on the corner, was the Hind and Pearl Pub. A faded painting of a large stag with a lovely damsel hung above the door and was the explanation for the name.

The pub was well-lit and more than half-full. Arthur found a table near the offside, away from the darts, and Melody sat there to wait for the men to return with their drinks. She looked around at the various patrons. Most were older, and she regarded them as being drawn more from the various houses and apartments in the area. They were probably arriving on foot since few cars were seen on the street.

The tweeds her cousin suggested she wear fit right in with the clientele. Most of the fabrics and colors were subdued, an indication that many of the wearers were either wealthy or had come from upper-class backgrounds. The brighter the tweed, the newer the money. She smiled, her tweed jacket and calf-length skirt had belonged to her grandmother, and now she was happy she had kept it and could wear it.

The men returned with the drinks, and they sat on either side of her. Melody looked at Alfred. "You must live close to Cousin Arthur if this is your local."

Alfred chuckled. "Haven't you told her? Arthur, you wound me!" He smiled at Melody. "I live on the same street as Arthur. Actually, two doors down and across the street. The house isn't quite as large as the double Arthur has, but it is very elegant and was used extensively during the time my parents were up in London."

"You need to come to supper while you're here and I'll give you a tour." Alfred eyed Arthur. "I'm sure the two of you would enjoy something more than a curry."

Arthur snapped back. "And who will do the meal? You live there alone and do your own cooking. Unless you have learned a trade, I think we're better off with take-out."

Alfred shot back, "Agree to come and you will see how entertaining in a London house should be done. You haven't had more than a breakfast in yours since your parents died. And no"—he turned to Melody—"I will not be cooking, I have someone else do that for me."

Melody smiled at the back and forth between the two. Since the first day she had seen the two together, the sight of their bickering reminded her of brothers vying over the same toy. Their digs and put-downs seemed to be born from familiarity. She wondered how much Alfred was tweaking Arthur's nose as opposed to how serious the jabs really were.

"I would like to see your house." Melody turned to her guardian. "Can't we go for supper just one time before I leave to go back to Houston?"

Alfred's smile faded. "Back to Houston. Why are you doing that?" He turned angrily to Arthur. "What have you done? Are you driving her away? You can't let her go!"

Arthur was surprised at the outburst. "Calm down. She wants to go for the American Thanksgiving holiday and she'll stay through Christmas, but she's coming back the second week of January, so there is nothing to get your knickers in a twist over. Besides, she's not your ward. She's mine, and I have given her my permission."

Melody would have said something, but the atmosphere between the two was already tense. She did want to ask about the coincidence of the two men having houses on the same street in such a large, populous city, but thought she would do that when alone with one of them, not the two.

Alfred asked if she wanted a refill, but Arthur had had enough of this evening and said as much. "Look, it's time we got back to the house. Tomorrow we have so much to do. If you really think you can put on a meal, we can be there after tomorrow."

Alfred beamed. "Excellent! So come about seven and we'll have drinks. Dinner will be at eight. Oh, and if you don't mind, there will be other people at the party."

Arthur frowned. "I thought just the three of us. Who are the other people? Can I see the guest list? I...I just don't know about this."

His opponent laughed. "Don't worry. I would never expose Melody to anyone not on society's 'approved' list. I'm not a complete cad."

Melody put her coat on and picked up her purse. "If you two are going to walk me back to the house, I am ready to go."

Alfred and Arthur walked in silence. At the bottom steps to Farr House, Alfred bid them both good night and continued on down the street and crossed before the end.

Melody told her cousin to have pleasant dreams and went to bed. Tomorrow was supposed to be a busy day, and she didn't want to miss it.

Lovely smells greeted Melody when she walked into the sunny breakfast room. Mrs. Jones was putting a plate of sausages, eggs, grilled tomatoes, and sautéed mushrooms in front of Cousin Arthur as she came in, and the young girl, Angie, was filling his coffee cup and setting out buttered toast. Mrs. Jones asked Melody what she would like and left to bring it to her.

Instead of taking the car, a black taxi was sitting at the foot of the stairs when Melody and Sir Arthur left the house. The two settled into the back and Cousin Arthur gave the man an address in Knightsbridge. Arthur explained the places they would be going would have zero parking available, and taking the car would be more trouble than it was worth.

The taxi stopped in front of a store with boots and shoes in the windows. Arthur opened the door to the shop for Melody, and the smell of tanned leather, boot polish, and saddle soap filled the air. It was a bootmaker's, probably one of the few left in London, and it was here where Arthur had his boots and shoes made. The owner of the shop greeted them with a big smile and showed the two to a couple of comfortable chairs. Around the room, discreetly placed, were seals of royal commissions. Melody and Arthur were in the shop where royal boots had been fashioned for more than one hundred years.

Arthur tried on a pair of short boots he had ordered a couple months before and found them, as usual, to his liking. Melody looked at a pair of almost finished calf- length riding boots in a soft cordovan leather. The feel was soft and buttery, but it was much too large for her tiny feet. A woman came and asked her what she was interested in, and Melody told her she would like some boots, but would not be available to have the lasts made nor fittings done until at least after the holidays.

The taxi was waiting on the street and the next stop was to Sir Arthur's tailor. For many people, Saville Row was the place in London to find the finest tailored suits, but her cousin had a man in a short street just off the Row that had been making his suits since he was in university. Today was a fitting, and Melody looked at the fabrics while Arthur was trying on his new jacket.

It was just after 11:00 a.m. and the taxi dropped the two back at the townhouse. Angie took the parcel from Arthur and put it in his room. Mr. Jones was in the dayroom with a coffee tray, sherry, and cherry cake. It was an old tradition in the late morning to have a glass of sherry, a slice of cherry cake, followed by a cup of coffee.

Unlike the cakes Melody was familiar with, the ones served with the sherry were not sweet, but had a bit of a tartness brought out by the cherries. It held the people partaking of it over until a proper luncheon was served at 1:00 p.m. or so.

After the cake and sherry, Arthur invited Melody on a tour of the second floor. She was happy to have a chance to see it.

"At the time the two houses were made into one, my great-grand parents did a lot of entertaining in London. This was also the age when large, weekly dinner parties were the norm, and at least once during the 'season' each house had a ball." On the second floor, Arthur slid the pocket doors open at the head of the landing to reveal a large room. He flipped the light switch, and a highly polished wood mosaic floor with a light coating of dust greeted them. Around the room were several chairs and in the front, a raised platform that would have accommodated a small string quartet or a group who would have played waltzes. Placed in strategic locations on the walls, ornate mirrors were hung to make the room look much larger. Even the Houston house didn't have a ballroom. Arthur backed out of the room, turned off the light, and quietly slid the doors closed. "It seems a waste, but it was their way of doing things. Now here we have another salon, next to it is a study and small library. Lavatory facilities were added later, and that is about it for this floor."

"Right now, I need to do some work in the study. If you want to putter around in the library, it is here." Arthur reached out and opened the door to an oak lined room with bookcases that were half-filled. "I will be done in about an hour then we can have lunch. This afternoon I have an appointment at my bank. We won't be far from some nice stores if you want to do some shopping. Think about it."

Without waiting for Melody to reply, Arthur left her in the library and walked into the study and closed the door. Sometimes her cousin could be so cryptic, but she didn't feel it was her place to question him.

During lunch a letter arrived for her cousin, and instead of putting it aside to read after the meal, he opened it immediately. Arthur had told her at the very beginning of her stay in Farr Cottage that there would be no reading, business, or cellular phone use at the table. "I've seen how you Americans are, and we do it differently here. "The letter must have been important for him to break his own rule.

Arthur frowned. "Hmmm, seems Alfred has a nice guest list for dinner tomorrow night. Well, we did say we would go, so I suppose it is on. I shall give him a call after lunch to confirm."

Melody smiled. It was nice to see the two getting on so much better. "If you like, I can call for you. You have your meeting and there isn't much for me to do but shop, and that doesn't thrill me." Her cousin nodded his assent.

Melody made the call to Alfred as soon as the lunch was finished. She accepted the invitation for her and her guardian, and when asked what her plans were for the day, Melody told Alfred about the shopping trip. "Let me meet you," Alfred said, "and I can show you some of the best places in London." Melody agreed, and they set a place and time to meet.

The taxi took Arthur and Melody to his bank and from there, Arthur gave the taxi instructions to take her to Harrods. "I am sure this is where you will find everything you could possibly wish to take back to Houston with you for your Christmas. We shall meet at the house for drinks at the usual time, five thirty, and from there we have dinner with the Marshalls so you'll want to dress for dinner out."

Once alone in the taxi, Melody called Alfred to let him know she was on her way to Harrods. He sent a text message back that he would meet her at the south entrance near the perfumes.

Melody had barely gotten into Harrods before Alfred was by her side. "Is there anything in particular you're looking for or just browsing? Maybe Christmas presents for your American friends?"

"I'm not really interested in anything at the moment. Most of my friends travel extensively and buy whatever they want. We don't give gifts to each other unless it is something unique they couldn't find for themselves. My family always gave to charity, worked at the church, or did things in the community. I suppose there has been little under our Christmas tree since I was a child."

"Well," Alfred asked, "if you're not here for presents, why are you here?"

Melody chuckled. "Mostly because Arthur sent me here in the taxi. I suppose he hasn't figured out I don't like to shop. I have friends that live for a mall or shopping center, but for me, if I can't buy it over the Internet, it's not worth getting." Alfred took her by the arm and steered her toward the door. "Then let's get out of here. Fancy a glass of wine or cup of tea?"

Within minutes, they were seated at a table in a posh pub near the store. Alfred stood at the bar getting a half- pint for himself and a glass of white wine for Melody.

"So, Melody Farr, why are you going back to Houston? I know what you said in the local, but tell me why you really want to leave your guardian's care."

The last, about her guardian's care, was said with a decided note of sarcasm. Melody took note and thought a few moments before answering. "I want to go home to my own house. This time of year was always special. Mother and I, and grandmother when she was still alive, loved this season the best."

She continued, "You see, Father died when I was young and it was just the three of us left. As long as grandmother was alive, the house was still fully staffed, but when she passed, mother found no need for live-ins. We had a girl— woman actually—who would come a couple of days a week, but it was just the two of us until Mother died. I just want to go back to my own room, my friends, and, well, my own life."

Alfred took her hand. "Then you're not happy here? What has that idiot done to turn you away?"

Melody could sense a rising anger in him and wanted to stop it before it got out of control. She took her hand back and looked him in the eye. "Arthur hasn't done anything. This is all me. I like my home, my life, my friends, and I miss them. That is the extent of the "problem" and nothing that my guardian has done."

His voice softened and he reclaimed her hand. "Will you come back, or is that just an assumption Arthur has made? I know how he can be, and seeing what is in front of him hasn't always been one of his strong points."

"I don't know. The work on the genealogy has been interesting and engrossing, but I'm not sure if it's something I want to continue for the rest of the time until I turn thirty. Marking days off on a calendar hasn't been one of my more joyous pursuits. I just don't know."

Alfred went to the bar for another half-pint and offered Melody a refill on the wine. She had put her hand over the glass before he left to refill his own drink. When he came back, they continued the conversation. "What *do* you want? You don't want to tick off days until you're thirty, settling into Farr Cottage doesn't seem to agree with you, so what do you want besides going to live in an old house by yourself with the family ghosts?"

This time Melody didn't just chuckle at the thought of "family ghosts" but laughed. "We have no ghosts. I sometimes think that is something that is pure English, the idea of an old house as being haunted. No, my house has no unsettled spirits. It was a house of love and family."

"You know, that little house that great-great grandfather Richard Farr built for his family is the only house that any of his issue has ever owned. Not one of his children, grandchildren, or great-grandchildren has ever felt like going out and building a house separate from what he had first built. Now, it has been expanded upon, partially rebuilt after a hurricane passed through, and upgraded with some better plumbing and electrical wiring, but it is still the home of all the American Farrs." She took the last sip of her wine. "After having seen Farr Cottage, I know we can't keep up with the long history of that place, but then, I don't need nor want to. What I have in Houston is enough for me. As to what I want, that is the short-term goal. In the long- term, I'm still working on that."

Alfred took her glass before she could object, "I promise, this is the last you'll have before I drop you at the house."

Melody watched him at the bar. He was asking some questions she had been occupied with asking herself as of late. Beyond her current plans, she still hadn't worked out the future, and as a "planner," she needed to get that right in her mind.

Her mother's death, the shock of the will, and the whole guardian thing just put her in an uncomfortable place. The people in her family didn't just decide "I am going to do this or that" without consulting the rest of the family. They weren't individuals as much as members of a whole. Her mother and grandmother had helped her decide the right college and university for her to attend. She had chosen the area of study, but not without first consulting her family. That is how decisions were made.

Now, she had to decide what was best for herself and for her future. Did it involve a husband? Well, that was an easy answer—yes—but it had to be the "right" husband. So far, she hadn't seen any really qualified candidates. But then, could she look while she was under the guardianship of the will? Would she want to choose someone just because the trustees found the man to be financially suitable without a criminal record? From what she knew about the process, that is not how you picked a husband, the father of future generations.

Alfred set her glass down and took his seat. "You look lost in thought. So you haven't yet decided what you want for your future. Is there a husband, children, pets, in that future, or will you become like Arthur, an aging historian, covered in more layers of dust than the books he reads?"

The last got Melody's attention. Arthur had never told her what he did for a living and hadn't told her he was a historian. "A historian? He never told me. We've worked in the same library for months, you would think he could have said something."

Alfred laughed. "Sounds like Arthur. He's been living in his own bubble for years, at least since he came down from Oxford. I suppose it's gotten worse since his parents passed. You know his mother died when he was at university and his father not long after? He does have a job though."

Melody nodded in the negative. "He has told me nothing. He spends his days in the library at a desk just near me, and there are also some trips he makes, but other than a couple of small dinner parties where he entertained people, he identified as 'business associates,' I've never known what he did."

Alfred made the decision to tell her; she had a right to know and for him, it was not something that was a secret. "He's called a *book*. I suppose he has told you how the Farr family has always served their king—well in this case, queen. Well, this is what he does. He works as a consultant to different ministries as a reference source."

"Book? I've never heard of the term. What does it mean?" Alfred chuckled. "*Book* is an old term. I suppose it comes from a time when not everyone could read or were educated. It just means someone who is recognized as a very learned person in a specific subject. For

Arthur, it is British history and in particular, little known facts. He is quite good at finding or knowing minutia but not 'seeing' what is in front of his face. Humph, and that is all we should say on the matter. It's time I got you back home so you can dress for dinner." Out on the street, he hailed a cab.

The black taxi they were riding in pulled to the curb in front of the townhouse. Alfred got out and opened Melody's door for her. "Remember, tomorrow evening you're having dinner at my house. I have some very interesting friends coming whom I would like to introduce you to, so please, if you brought one with you, a long gown would be wonderful. Arthur also knows it's black-tie."

He waited on the street until the door to the townhouse opened and Melody disappeared inside, then he paid the driver and walked to his house. Alfred wasn't sure just how he felt about the girl. She was beautiful, smart, and quite self-contained. He was convinced she could take care of herself, but this thing with her father's will, well, that was something else.

Originally, she was just someone new in the neighborhood and presented an oddity for him to befriend or at least acquaint himself with while he had to be in the country. He was surprised she looked like she did.

Small villages were hotbeds of gossip, and she had been the main topic from the day Arthur had been contacted about being her guardian. Most of the gossip was concerned with the fact she was twenty-eight and unmarried. Something had to be wrong with her. Everyone knew the contents of the will as it pertained to the need for a guardian, but not the extent of the estate the will was designed to protect. Why would a father think it necessary to write such a clause if he could trust his child or children not to be spendthrifts of a small inheritance? It baffled the locals and intrigued Alfred.

Having gotten to know the girl, however, she didn't seem to have the habits the will was designed to guard against, so his opinion was the father was worried his daughter would be the target of unscrupulous suitors. Friends of his in Houston were familiar with the family, but only second- and third-hand. According to them, they were rather dull and stayed to themselves, almost bordering on the reclusive. So she was going back to that life. Did he care? For some reason he couldn't quite understand, he did. Barring what Arthur thought, she was probably his only living relative, besides Arthur, and what happened to her could mean the continuance of his line into the future. He needed time to think about the ramifications of her. After all, perhaps there was hope for his future.

Alfred slipped the key in the lock on his door. Funny, his father and mother never carried keys to their houses or cars. They always had a butler to open the door when they came home and a chauffeur to drive them. When they died so suddenly in the Alps, he had released the staff, but not before his father's last butler found the key to the front door.

————))◉((————

Melody looked at her watch as she waited for the door to be opened to her knock. Angie, Mrs. Jones's niece, responded.

Angie had been dusting and airing the house. "Miss, is there anything I can do for you before I leave? Aunt Midge, uh, Mrs. Jones, just left but will be back to make breakfast in the morning. Is there something special you want or need?" "Thank you, Angie, but no, nothing. Is my cousin back yet?"

"Oh yes, he is, but he's upstairs getting dressed for dinner. He had me put the drinks cart in the salon though, so I guess you'll have something before you go out. So, if there is nothing else, I'm off."

Melody wished her a good evening and went to her room to change. Her cousin told her a short cocktail dress was fine for the dinner, and her favorite "little black dress" with the pearls she had inherited from her grandmother would do wonderfully.

While she dressed and fixed her hair, she thought about her meeting with Alfred. It still amazed her how alike the two men were, her cousin and Alfred, but how much animosity there was between them. Neither man wanted to let her in on the cause of their discord, but she was sure it had something to do with people long dead.

This house, Farr Cottage, all of it, too many secrets. Perhaps this was one of the reasons she needed to get back to her own house, her own life.

Err...

Arthur stood at the drinks cart making her a whiskey when Melody entered the room. "So how was your afternoon? Find anything interesting?"

"Well, actually, the only thing interesting was a glass of wine with Alfred. When I called him this afternoon, he asked to join me and since shopping is not really something I do, we sat and had a drink with our conversation."

Melody saw the frown on Arthur as soon as she mentioned Alfred's name. Granted, it wasn't as bad as when she had first gotten to Farr Cottage, but it was still there.

"And what did the two of you find to talk about?" Arthur said with some peevishness in his voice. "Has the boy found a job yet, or is he still living off the trust?"

"It wasn't his job we talked about, even though I doubt he would tell me if he had changed jobs. No, it was yours."

Arthur's head snapped up. "What did he tell you, little brat, it's not his place to talk about me!"

"Oh, just that you were a historian, a 'book' is what he called you, and I don't know why you're angry. I find it interesting, the work you do. However, he couldn't really tell me any details, so there's nothing for you to be mad about. I wish you had told me, but then it's not really my business." Melody turned and sat on the overstuffed sofa. "Besides, it's too nice an evening to worry about Alfred."

Arthur calmed down and set his glass on the side table. "Really, my work is very boring for anyone not into obscure facts. At university, I found a use for my photographic memory. It seems every book I have ever read or journal article is stuck in my head. A professor at Oxford helped me learn to sort all these dusty little facts into a kind of cerebral filing cabinet that lets me recall things in a more orderly manner. In fact, it was this professor that recommended me for my current job with the government. Several ministries use my services at different times."

"Anyway, it's time we left. Finish your drink and let's go or we'll be late, and I am never 'fashionably late.' Such a horrible idea, a Victorian invention I think. Come, the taxi is probably already here."

Arthur held her coat for her and locked the door behind them. The taxi was at the curb, and they made the short trip to the Marshall's in silence.

A uniformed maid opened the door as Arthur and Melody stepped off the elevator. Melody guessed the doorman had called ahead to let the Marshalls know they had guests coming. The girl took Melody's coat, bag, Arthur's overcoat, and scarf.

Light laughter and conversation could be heard coming from the salon, and Arthur steered Melody toward the room. Hilly Marshall greeted them both and sent Arthur off to talk to Frank. Hilly took Melody in hand and began the introductions.

Most of the women in the room were in their late middle years, and the men were mostly Melody's age. It took only two introductions before she realized the women were the mothers and the sons were there to meet her. George, Harold, and Charles were the guests the Marshalls were so anxious to introduce to Melody.

George was only twenty-eight and although the youngest of the three, had already started balding. He was an investment banker in the city. His constant attention to his cell phone was annoying and made conversation very difficult.

Harold was pudgy, round, and must have suffered from bad feet. His first inclination was to find a comfortable sofa where he could nurse a glass of sherry. Melody was surprised when his mother told her he was only thirty-two because he seemed much older. He looked so uncomfortable Melody was almost sorry for him.

Charles was the last possible suitor, and that is what they were, to be introduced. He had hung back waiting for the first two men to make their impressions. Melody watched him observing her and wondered what he was thinking. His impassive expression gave nothing away, but the light in his eyes told her his brain was not on idle.

Charles Edward Allen was tall, blond, and very handsome. Compared to the other two men, he was a Norse god. His dinner jacket was impeccably cut; he had strong features, and emerald green eyes. At thirty-five, he was the oldest of the offerings.

Melody watched as Hilly slipped out to the dining room, and Melody guessed Hilly had changed seating arrangements. Charles had a smooth voice, lovely manners, and Melody didn't trust him a bit. One thing she learned growing up in Houston was the chances the man standing in front of her was what he portrayed to her were slim to none. She hadn't dated a lot, but when she did, she had been told to watch for the boys—and later, men—who were wanting something from her, and her antenna told her Charles and his mother were in that category.

Arthur and Frank observed from a corner of the room until it was time to go into dinner. As each young man and his hopeful mother were introduced, Arthur watched for a flicker, a twitch, anything that would indicate there was any interest. So far, nothing. Everyone was on their supreme polite, best behavior, but that was as far as it went. No sparks, no lightening strikes of even the slightest interest. The men could have been the latest science experiments for all the effect they had on Melody.

Frank shook his head. "Well, it is short notice. Hilly did a quick run-through of her address book and without really knowing the girl, this was the selection which is available and in town at the moment. Sorry, but you did say she would be back after the first of the year. Perhaps with more time."

"Maybe, it was a long shot, but Melody sprang this on me in the last few days. Please keep looking. There just might be someone out and about that would keep her interest here." Arthur turned to set his drink on the table as the maid called the party into dinner.

Melody was escorted to dinner by the handsome Charles. She didn't know him, but something about him just didn't click. It couldn't be because he was trying too hard—he wasn't—nor was it his pushy mother. No, she would think of it.

Hilly had, either by chance or design, put her next to Charles at the dinner table. George was across from her and Harold next to him. She was surrounded. She had given, planned, and attended many dinner parties, and the seating arrangement for this one was all wrong. Where people would be seated to keep conversation moving, men and women mixed for balance, and the focus on the whole table and not just one part, this party didn't follow any of those guidelines.

She was the main attraction, and the rest of the guests were just there for the food.

Melody was very aware of the reason for the dinner, and the look she gave her cousin let him know she knew he was the one responsible. However, her manners did not fail her, and the dinner was enjoyed in spite of the original intentions.

Harold, or Harry as he insisted being called, was a researcher at the British Museum in their Egyptian collections department. Charles didn't say much, but his mother was quick to say he managed the family biscuit firm. George was actually quite funny when he finally put down his cell phone and joined the conversation. His description of a recent merger had everyone laughing. Melody thanked the Marshalls for a lovely dinner before she and Arthur left. No phone numbers were exchanged or appointments to meet made. By ten thirty, Arthur and Melody were back at the house and both decided a nightcap was in order.

London weather, the rainy kind, greeted Melody the next day when she dressed and joined Arthur for breakfast. Arthur was not planning to go out before the dinner at Alfred's that evening. Her cousin had work to do in the library and was spending the day at home.

Melody had thought she would find something to do in the meantime, but by midmorning, she was bored. She called Alfred and asked him what he recommended. He immediately invited her to have lunch with him.

Arthur barely grunted his acknowledgement when Melody told him she would be going out. Alfred was crossing the street as she exited onto the street. "Are you sure you don't need to be at home to prepare for your guests this evening?"

Alfred laughed. "No, that is why I have staff. Dinner is in hand and I don't have to be back until it's time to change. Now, it seems to me you need to see more of London and if left to Arthur, the only thing you'll see is the inside of his library. Come, I've called a taxi and"—He looked down the street, a cab rounded the corner—"it looks like it's here."

Alfred gave the driver an address and they settled into the back-seat. "When I was a child, my nanny used to take me to lunch at a lovely restaurant near Hyde Park. I thought we would go there and then do a little sightseeing. Interested?" Melody nodded her assent and they were off. Even with the rain, the city was beautiful. Alfred pointed to some interesting sights and some she recognized without being told.

The Inn on the Park was a fine-looking hotel, and the restaurant overlooking the park was not quite full. Both ate light because dinner would be multi-course and Melody wanted to be able to enjoy the food. As she thought about it, she had never seen Alfred eat much, and he also didn't on this occasion.

"I had hoped the rain would have let up so we could walk in the park for a bit, but it looks like the weather will not cooperate. How about a quick taxi tour and then we can get some down time before the evening?"

Melody agreed, and Alfred told the taxi driver where he wanted to go on the way home.

The short taxi tour took them past Buckingham Palace, Parliament, and Whitehall. Melody recognized all of them from pictures she had seen in books, but the reality of them was breathtaking. She felt like a kid as she sat open mouthed and in awe at their splendor. Seeing London like this made it even more tempting to see other places about which she had only read. The tour, however, was all too brief before the cab left her and Alfred at the steps of her cousin's townhouse.

Alfred bid her good-bye. The same girl who had been at the door the day before, Angie, greeted Melody as she went up the steps of the townhouse. Melody soundlessly opened the door to the library and Arthur acknowledged her with a grunt as she told her cousin hello. He wasn't even aware she had been out.

In her room, she puttered around with her laptop for a while before starting her preparations for drinks with Arthur before the dinner with Alfred. A leisurely bath, an up-do for the hair, and a bare minimum of makeup; she was ready for her favorite dress.

The dove-grey charmeuse silk dress she wore fit Melody like a second skin. She topped it with a matching dupioni- silk jacket that had an iridescence that caught the light as she moved. A string of grey pearls was the only jewelry, and the whole look was stunning.

Arthur had dressed in a tuxedo, a relic from his father, that had been the style in the 1960s. The antique look of the suit worked very well with the dress Melody wore and made the pair look more vintage Rat Pack than modern London. A playing of Frank Sinatra recordings would have completed the scene.

Again, Arthur was struck by the quiet beauty of his ward. He had begun noticing her more and more these last few weeks. Where most women he saw dressed either in dowdy outfits or clothes more suitable for a hooker, he was happy to see his ward consistently appear in classic ensembles appropriate to a young lady of means. She had taste, and the figure to wear the clothes without the clothes wearing her.

Arthur locked the front door and put the key in his pocket. He turned and took Melody's arm as they both descended the front stairs of the townhome. Across the street, at Alfred's house, a taxi had just pulled to the curb. A young couple emerged, and Arthur and Melody were in time to join them as the front door opened and Daws, the Oswin family's retired butler, greeted the guests.

Arthur spoke to Daws as the butler took his coat and a uni-formed maid accepted Melody's coat and purse. The weather had cleared and although the rain had stopped, the temperature had dropped. Since the house felt comfortably warm, Melody also relinquished the jacket that matched the dress.

Alfred greeted the couple who had preceded Arthur and Melody through the door and then turned to his neighbors. As Melody removed her jacket, Alfred was the first to get the full impression of just how well the grey silk fit her figure.

Alfred kept his focus on Melody as he shook Arthur's hand. Arthur followed Alfred's gaze. In a defining moment, Arthur saw more than his ward but a very desirable woman. He also recognized the same look in Alfred's eyes. Melody, however, was unaware of the impact she had made.

The two men kept their attention on Melody long enough to understand they would be competing against each other and also against all other eligible males either at the dinner party or anywhere else she might be. The two men who had been at odds most of their lives now had a common goal, but they both realized Melody's trip home to Houston would take her away just when each man wanted her near.

Alfred looked around the salon at the men and women gathered for his dinner party. None of the couples were married. All of the men and women were eligible bachelors and bachelorettes who attended parties, vacations, or house parties as a group. It was understood by all that eventually each of the men would find one of the women in the crowd as suitable to marry, and as they had reached their late twenties or early thirties, would do just that. Bringing Melody into this equation had seemed like a good idea, but now he thought differently.

The party of men and women knew Arthur, but none had seen the American girl. The members of this roving band of friends were all from the same social strata, and if it hadn't been for her last name and the sponsorship, as it were, of her standing by both Arthur and Alfred, Melody might not have been received as suitable to join the pack.

As a good host, Alfred took Melody's arm and guided her around the room, introducing her to each of the guests. A couple of the women showed a twinge of jealousy, but the men were eager to make her acquaintance. Halfway around the room, the doorbell rang and Alfred had to leave Melody with John Sloan and Alice Godsell.

John and Alice immediately took up the introductions. Both worked in advertising, and John was especially taken by the American girl's fresh look. He asked Melody if she had ever done any modeling, but Alice was quick to admonish him with a reminder this was a social event, not a business dinner.

A liveried waiter came with a tray of drinks and Melody accepted her usual whiskey. The couple Alfred had greeted seemed to be the last to join, and Melody counted twenty- four people. Alfred and Arthur stood on each side of her as she talked to various guests, but when the doors to the dining room were opened and Daws called dinner, it was Alfred who insisted on taking Melody's arm. With Melody seated on his right and Arthur on his left, the rest of the party found their place cards.

Melody smiled at her host. "Alfred, your dining room is the first I have seen that would be a match for the one in my home in Houston."

The reference to Houston and Melody's impending trip refocused both Alfred and Arthur. The gentleman seated on the other side of Melody, Nicolas Somersby, also heard a reference to Houston and asked Melody about her home. Melody could feel the tension between Arthur and Alfred. From the first time she had seen them together, she had been struck by how awkward their interaction had been—but this was different. The two men glowered at each other and beamed at her. It was uncomfortable, and she chose to ignore the two by concentrating on the man to her right.

Nicky Somersby was an architect and childhood friend of Alfred. He told Melody that most of the people, men and women, sitting around the table were longtime mates. Melody had understood from a couple of the people she had talked to before dinner that the group had either gone to school together, public or university, or been friends through their parents.

Melody asked Nicky what kind of work he did, and it was his cue to tell her all about himself. "Currently I design conversions and restorations. A few years back, when the London council decided to refurbish the Thames, one of the things they did was stop much of the shipping into the port of London and moved it downriver. It has helped clean the river, but it left a lot of docks and warehouses empty and useless. This is when some of the owners decided to repurpose the buildings into lofts for housing."

"In the beginning," he continued, "there were ten lofts for every one buyer, but now it's one loft for every ten buyers. People saw the space, the views, and the convenience they got with a docklands loft and it made them rare finds." He motioned to the head of the table. "Alfred here has some of the last un-reclaimed warehouse property that has not been converted, and this is what he and I are doing now.

I think all of the space has been spoken for, and the work is still in the design stage."

Melody waited for the server to take her plate and put a salad in front of her. "Is that the only thing you do? Lofts?" Nicky laughed. "No, over the last few years we've done two rows of houses on the near-East end, a couple duplexes in Chelsea, and three houses just off Harley Street. And, as far as I know, Alfred has some other properties he will be having me do in the future."

Melody put her fork down. "And all of those you have done with Alfred?"

Nicky nodded, but before he could continue, Alfred broke into the conversation. "This is what keeps me busy. I told you my 'job' was managing what I had been left when Mother and Father had their crash. Well, this is a great part of it."

Alfred continued, "When I was about ten, I had come home during a term break from school. Mother and father couldn't meet me at the train because they had an 'important' luncheon for clients of my father. It angered me. By the time the housekeeper fetched me from the train, the luncheon was over, mother had gone to her room to rest before she and father would go out in the evening, and father was in his study. I knew not to disturb mother when she was resting, but I did go in to say hello to my father. I let him know I was not happy."

Alfred took a sip of his wine and went on, "Father took me by the hand and he walked me outside to the sidewalk. He pulled a five-pound note from his pocket and laid it on the pavement. He told me, 'Son, this five-pound note will not pay for the land it covers. Nowhere in London will a five-pound note pay for what it covers. Now, if you were to take this fiver into the house and lay it down on the floor in the servants-quarters, it wouldn't even pay for the floor- covering.' By this time I was beginning to understand, but he wanted to finish his point. 'Alfred,' he said to me, 'some of my people pay me in money, some in other valuables, and some in property. Today it was agreed I would receive some property. This is for your future and the future of the family, so it's high time you appreciated that work is not something I do because I like it more than my wife and child—no, it's something I do so we all live well now and in the future." I just look after and expand what he started." Alfred looked around the room. The chatter at the table had quieted when Alfred had first started talking. Many of the men and women at the table could relate to having similar closeness to their parents.

"Nicky, we start the dock project in the New Year, but maybe you should also get busy with doing a refurbish of this place and Aldwin House. I'm thinking it might be time for me to see about getting married and having some children of my own." Alfred said.

Melody was looking at her cousin while Alfred was saying the last bit about getting married, and the look on his face went from horror to anger. Although she didn't understand why, it made her think it did not bode well for relations between the two men. Two other ladies at the table also took more than a passing interest in what had been said.

Beryl Somersby, sister to Nicky, and Maude Harbison had both shown an interest in Alfred through the years, but neither knew of the other's attentiveness. Now, however, it looked like Alfred had come to the realization that it was time to get on with life, and both women thought they could make him into a good husband. Beryl was a couple of years younger than Nicky and a year older than Maude was. Each had good educations, careers, and if Alfred were ready to find a wife, either girl would be ready to be the results of his hunt.

Arthur knew whom Alfred was talking about even if it had escaped Beryl and Maude. Now he wished he had included Melody in his plans for Paris, but he hadn't and although he would like to spend more time with her to press his own case, perhaps her trip home was just the thing to get her away from Alfred. He would arrange it all in the morning.

The rest of the evening was a blur for the two men. Both sat next to Melody for coffee and brandy in the drawing room. Alfred took Melody's arm as Arthur and Melody prepared to leave. Alfred even helped Melody with her jacket and coat as she dressed warmly for the walk across the street. And, for the first time, he kissed Melody's cheek when he wished them a good night.

Arthur watched it all with dread. He took Melody's arm as they walked the short distance to the house. In the foyer, he helped her off with her coat and invited her to stay by the fire in the lounge and have another brandy. Melody pled tiredness and said good night. Alone, with a short brandy in his hand, Arthur wished he had taken the opportunity to plant his own kiss good night on her cheek and railed against himself for having let her slip away without his doing so.

———— >«(●)»‹ ————

Sun streamed through the breakfast room windows as Melody joined Arthur for their last meal in London. Arthur pulled an envelope from his inner pocket and handed it to his ward.

"I have made reservations for your trip back to Farr Cottage and then on to Houston. The details are inside along with the tickets. Is two days at the Cottage time enough for you to pack what you need for the trip? Oh, if not, just call the agency whose number is on the itinerary, and they can make any adjustments."

Melody looked at the contents of the packet. She didn't like the air carrier, but she would make those changes later. At one point she had worried Arthur would not like to see her go, but now it seemed he couldn't wait to get rid of her. *Hmmm,* she thought, *why the change?*

"I will be going to Paris shortly after you leave here today. So, after breakfast, pack your things. I suppose Angie can give you a hand if you need it, but as you see, your train is at eleven and you wouldn't want to miss it."

Melody put the papers back in the envelope. "I can pack for myself, cousin. If you don't mind, I will change the carrier for the trip to Houston and give myself an upgrade on the seating. On such a long flight, more legroom is preferable. Don't worry, I will cover the cost out of my monthly stipend." Her cousin mumbled something and Melody continued, "Will you be back from Paris before I leave, or is this good-bye until January?"

Arthur was struck by the idea.

**Good-bye until January. Did he really want
to let her go?**

www.ingramcontent.com/pod-product-compliance
Lightning Source LLC
Chambersburg PA
CBHW060541130626
46553CB00002B/858